# STEP-BY-STEP
# printmaking

A Complete Introduction to the Craft of Relief Printing

**By Erwin Schachner**

Conceived and edited by
**William and Shirley Sayles**

 **GOLDEN PRESS · NEW YORK**

WESTERN PUBLISHING COMPANY, INC.
Racine, Wisconsin

# Foreword

Print, the mark left on a surface by pressure—the footprint on a beach, the imprint of a leaf or texture of weathered wood. Making a permanent record of an object, and making a series of like impressions that differ in color or surface texture, is only part of the intriguing craft of the printmaker. For the making of a print can be done in a wide variety of methods. These methods are graphically illustrated in the following pages.

The excitement resulting from the use of tools, materials, and techniques to achieve a print is also concisely demonstrated in this step-by-step presentation.

Erwin Schachner knows his subject from long experience with his own private press. His ideas have developed from the things that happen in the process of printmaking. In other words, his approach is based on day-to-day practice rather than theory.

The wide range of his work is represented by illustrations for books, magazines and advertising, as well as prints for the collector. His wood and linoleum prints may be seen in U.S. Information Service installations and American embassies around the world and as part of the "Europe One" exhibition of American printmakers.

I have enjoyed the stimulation of his creative prints in the gallery as well as the pleasure of working with a "professional" on demanding assignments for book work.

In this book you have an ideal guide through the practical craft disciplines which lead to the rewards of this creative medium. Not only will you learn how to make prints but you will also gain an expanded appreciation of the prints of others.

JOHN BEGG
*Art Director (1939–1968),*
*Oxford University Press*

*Library of Congress Catalog Card Number: 70–103422*

Linocut by Erwin Schachner

# Contents

### ACKNOWLEDGMENTS

Among those who have assisted in the preparation of this book, special thanks are due to:

Remo Cosentino, *Design and Production*
Louis Mervar, *Photography*
André J. Chodat, *Diagrams*

Woodcut print from the Nuremberg Chronicles published about 1493. Hand-colored over key block print, probably with stencils. Collection of Mary Walker Phillips.

# Introduction

The mark, line, or figure that the printmaker makes depends on tastes, needs, or interests and can range widely and wildly, for printing is a very personal pursuit. Each new piece of work is a challenge and from each there is something to learn.

Good prints can be made with simple tools and materials—a knife to carve a design out of a potato, ink to supply the color, and paper to receive the impression; or a wooden spoon to rub an impression from a raised inked surface onto a sheet of paper. You can create woodcuts, linoleum cuts, and wood engravings. You can print them by hand or on your own press. But it is not simply the creation of these printing materials that has made printmaking so fascinating to so many—there is a special feeling in the art of creating them. There is excitement and tension when that first cut or gouge is to be made into the surface of a smooth piece of linoleum or a block of wood. There is a gradual refinement of the tactile and visual senses as you explore the textured surfaces of paper with your hand, or rub a fine wood, admiring its grain, or select an individual type face, or realize how the look of ink alters with different papers.

You can work with type alone or in combination with linecuts, using the simplest equipment—and you can make more than one copy of your work. Much of the fascination of printing is in its wide variety of possibilities. As your skill and understanding grow, you will think of many ways to use this craft, for no one yet has discovered all the possible combinations of type, design, color, and method. Whether you decide to experiment with an elaborate print in five colors or get your satisfaction from a perfectly designed page of type, printing for pleasure is, as it has been for centuries, an outlet for the most personal and meaningful self-expression.

## RELIEF PRINTING

Of the print processes, relief printing, or printing from raised surfaces, is the oldest method, and the one with which we will be concerned in this book. It is the same method referred to by commercial printers as "letterpress"—the pressing of a letter against paper.

Relief printing is simple and direct. When a relief surface is covered with ink and a piece of paper is pressed upon it, the character of that surface will reproduce on the paper. A surface is in relief when

"Cryes of Londontown," 24″ x 26″, by Erwin Schachner. In two colors on antique stock. One of the pleasures of making a print is displaying it in your home.

"Floral Hunting Scene," 55½'' x 67½'', by Shiko Munakata. Woodcut. Printed in black and grey. Collection of the Museum of Modern Art, New York. Gift of the Felix and Helen Juda Foundation.

it is higher than the surrounding areas; and since ink cannot reach the lower areas, only the relief surface prints. Such a surface is made by cutting away all areas that are not meant to print.

## A LITTLE BACKGROUND

**Woodcuts.** Printing was practiced in China as early as the sixth century A.D.—nearly 900 years before it became known in Europe—when an imperial decree ordained that various texts should be engraved on wood to be printed and published. It was not until paper came to be manufactured in Europe in the 14th century—it had already been in use in China for 1,500 years—that woodcuts came into wide use.

Those early woodcuts were devoted to holy images which were created and sold by monks. Crudely cut and brightly colored, these representations of incidents from the life of Christ and favorite saints were bought by travelers making religious pilgrimages through Europe. Playing cards were also first produced at this time.

**Type**. The first major development in printing came to the Western world in the 15th century with Gutenberg's press, which was modeled on the winepresses of that period. Gutenberg used crude movable type in his press. The Chinese, however, were using movable type more than 400 years before Gutenberg. It was during a period in China when printing had reached its fullest development, under the Sung dynasty, that a blacksmith named Pe Ching introduced movable type. He made a paste of fine clay onto which he engraved type characters. After arranging them in an iron frame, he pressed a wooden board over them to ensure an even surface for printing. This process is identical to two steps in printing today—placing type in a form and planing it down. After printing, he was able to loosen the type and use it again.

At the same time that Gutenberg was using movable type, books were being produced in the Netherlands and in Germany which combined pictures and accompanying text, drawn and cut on the same plank. These "block books" were small, no larger than pam-

Frontispiece by Henri Matisse. Linocut. An example of the use of prints in book illustration. Collection of the Museum of Modern Art, New York. Gift of Abby Aldrich Rockefeller.

H. DE MONTHERLANT

# PASIPHAÉ
CHANT DE MINOS

*(LES CRÉTOIS)*

*Gravures originales par*

HENRI MATISSE

MARTIN FABIANI, EDITEUR

phlets. Although their production was a laborious process, it paid the publisher to engrave the text and pictures rather than use movable type, which was available only in limited amounts and was too soft to be durable. When movable type improved, the block book rapidly disappeared.

**Wood Engraving.** The technique of relief printing rose to new heights of refinement in the 16th century in the hands of Albrecht Dürer and his contemporaries, who abandoned bright colors in favor of exquisitely detailed drawings. It was two centuries later that Thomas Bewick, an Englishman, began a new phase by his use of white lines in delicate wood engravings. In these the design was engraved into the wood, whose main surface was left at its original level and then inked. As a result, the design printed out in white lines, permitting subtle shadings as opposed to the broad linear quality of woodcuts. Animals were Bewick's speciality and his famous book, the *General History of Quadrupeds,* which appeared in 1790, marked an epoch in the history of wood engravings. The press on which *Quadrupeds* was printed was very much the same as the one used by

*(Below)* One of a series from *Aesop's Fables.* Designed, cut, and printed by Joseph Low (Eden Hill Press). Linocut. An example of a printed piece produced by a private press. The print is attached to inside of fold.

AESOP: *A Lion in Love*

A LION was in love with a country lass, and desired her father's consent to have her in marriage. The answer he gave was churlish enough. He'd never agree to it, he said, upon any terms, to marry his daughter to a beast. The lion gave him a sour look which brought the bumpkin, upon second thoughts, to strike up a bargain with him, upon these conditions: that his teeth should be drawn and his nails pared; for those were things, he said, that the foolish girl was terribly afraid of. The lion sends for a surgeon immediately to do the work (as what will not love make a body do?) and so soon as the operation was over, he goes and challenges the father upon his promise. The countryman, seeing the lion disarmed, plucked up a good heart, and with a swinging cudgel so ordered the matter that he broke off the match.

*This is part of one print in the fourth Eden Hill Press publication: a portfolio of Aesop's fables, translated by Roger L'Estrange.*

"Bust of a Woman with a Hat," 25½" x 21", by Pablo Picasso. Linocut. One block. From *Picasso Linocuts 1958–1963*, by Donald H. Karshan, Tudor Publishing Co. Collection of the Computer Applications Inc.

(*Above*) Making a hand-rubbed print. The sheet on the inked block is rubbed with a wooden Japanese paddle.

(*Below*) Finished print is carefully peeled from the inked block.

Gutenberg to produce his Bibles, for during that period of three hundred years there had been almost no improvement of the presses.

**Private Presses.** These three centuries did, however, see the rise of private or "little" presses. These early presses were established either because of the scarcity of printers or because printing in general was under political and religious control. From there, expansion into printing for the sheer pleasure of it was a natural development. Benjamin Franklin, a printer by trade, began a private press during the time he was the American ambassador to France, using it to print official documents and sometimes items for his friends.

Private presses have often begun quite casually. One such, which subsequently produced four volumes, started because its owner happened to be at an auction when printing equipment was being sold. The ownership of a private press offers the opportunity for creative, unfettered experiments in the use of type. Thanks to such type designers as Garamond, Baskerville, Caslon, and Bodoni, to mention just a few, the appearance of the printed page tells a story of its own by complementing, highlighting or enhancing the text and pictures.

**Prints.** In recent years, the print has reached a new level of popularity. More and more people are discovering that they can express themselves in this medium. Print exhibitions have become events to go to, and editions of prints are being ordered in increasing numbers. It is in that spirit that we invite you to embark on an adventure which will expand your horizons and extend your imagination no matter what your age or occupation. Printmaking and printing have intrigued amateurs and professionals for hundreds of years. From anonymous monk to modern master, they have all joined the ranks of the many men and women who know the joy of having "printer's ink" in their blood.

**This Book.** For those who are new to printmaking, this book includes printing techniques to use without a press. Each section of the book describes a material—such as ink, paper, type—and how to use it, or a technique—woodcuts, linocuts, wood engravings—and how to apply it. Diagrams and illustrations throughout will help to take you step-by-step into various phases of printmaking. Also included is how to make a register board and how to use it for producing prints in good color registration. For those who want to work on presses, there are two comprehensive sections on the proof press and the platen press.

At the conclusion of the book you will find a glossary of terms for easy reference, a bibliography, and a list of suppliers for materials and equipment. Also included are schools and workshops where courses in printmaking are offered.

"Whale," 9" x 8½", by 10-year-old Alexis D. Kostich. Linocut. One color on Japanese paper.

# *Workshop*

Printmaking, like most crafts, requires some set-aside space in which to work effectively. This work area can be arranged according to your particular needs, interests, and the space you have available. As far as possible, however, everything related to the designing of printed pieces and the preparing of blocks should be arranged conveniently around or near the worktable (diagram **A**), while everything related to hand prints should be arranged on a separate inking table (diagram **C**). In the inking table diagrammed, the surface is that of a type cabinet with a glass slab for inking and various brayers, or rollers, close at hand.

You can produce perfectly good work with simple equipment, as in rubbing, offsetting, stamping, etc. This is demonstrated in "Printing Without a Press" (pages 36 to 45). However, as your interest in this

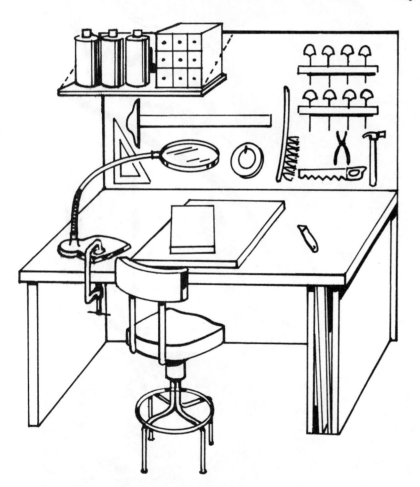

**A** Work area for designing printed pieces and preparing blocks.

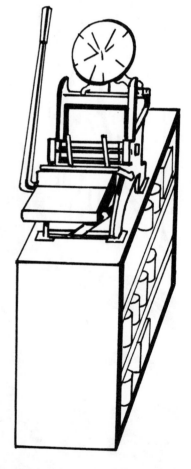

**B** Table model platen press, mounted on cabinet base with shelves for supplies.

medium grows, and you want to print on a larger scale, you might consider the purchase of a press. Both presses shown here, the platen press and the proof press, are table models set on cabinets. The cabinets have shelves for storing equipment.

The workshop shown is meant as a suggestion and aid for your own plans. Certain considerations are important, however. The worktable should be strong enough to withstand any hand pressure applied while cutting blocks of linoleum or wood. You should also be able to sit at a comfortable height to plan your designs. All tools relating to the work you are doing should be conveniently at hand. Neatness is important as well as handy storage. Work can be held up if you have to stop to find a brayer or a cutting tool. Everything that is not in use should be stored away. The inking table should be high enough so that you do not have to stoop when working on your hand prints.

An arrangement for hanging prints to dry is also needed. It may not be necessary to hang prints that have been made with a water-based ink since they dry so quickly, but those made with an oil-based ink will require a drying period. A double line of either rope or wire can be devised (such as the one suggested in the diagram), or a wooden rack can be used. Clip-type clothespins or metal clamps hold the prints perpendicular to the line.

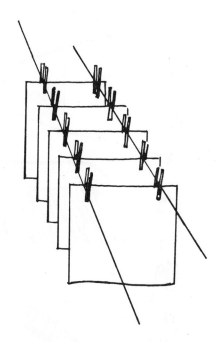

Rack for hanging and drying prints.

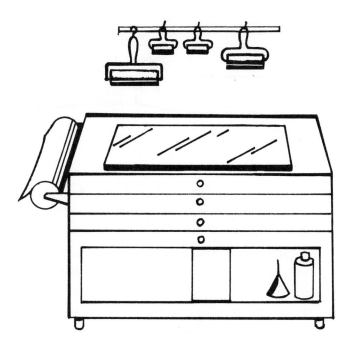

**C** Type cabinet with glass slab for inking. Drawers are type cases. Various-sized brayers hang conveniently within reach.

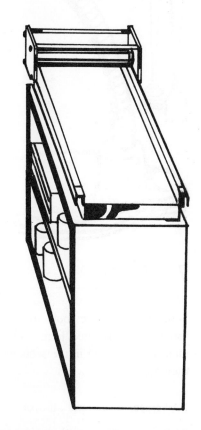

**D** Table model proof press mounted on storage cabinet base.

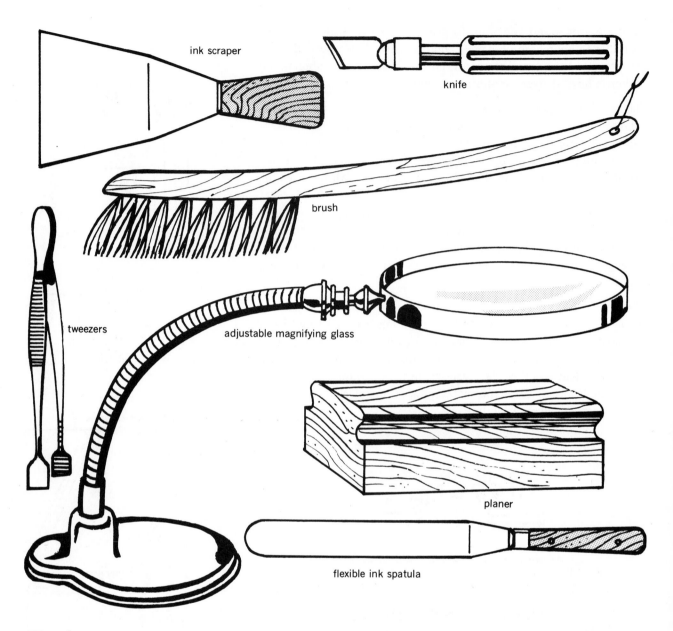

ink scraper

knife

brush

tweezers

adjustable magnifying glass

planer

flexible ink spatula

## *Tools*

Some of the basic tools used in printmaking are listed and illustrated here. Other tools and equipment are included in the sections of the book where they apply.

**Ink Scraper**—a general all-around tool.

**Knife**—all-purpose, with replaceable blades for scoring linoleum, and for cutting mats and cardboard.

**Brush**—long-handled. A handy tool for brushing away cuttings from wood and linoleum blocks, and for general cleaning.

**Adjustable Magnifying Glass**—used when cutting small detailed areas in wood or linoleum. Indispensable when doing a wood engraving.

**Planer**—for leveling small type in preparation for printing.

**Flexible Ink Spatula,** or palette knife—for mixing and spreading ink on glass slab.

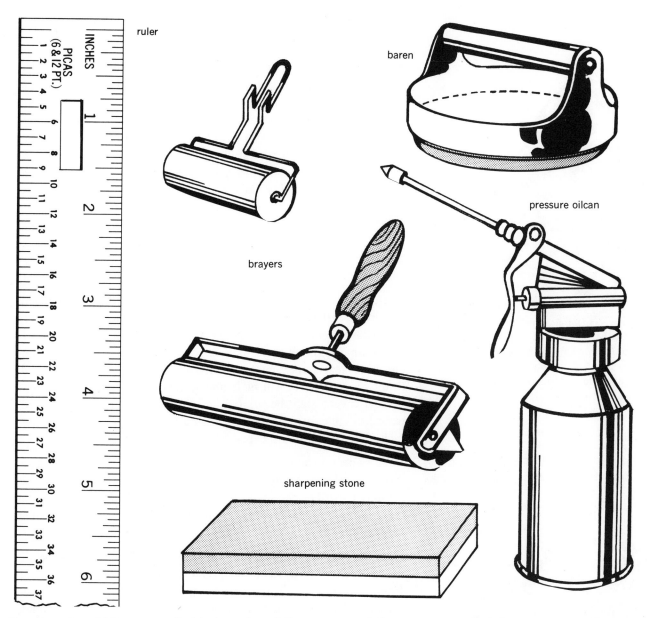

ruler

brayers

baren

pressure oilcan

sharpening stone

**Tweezers**—for picking up small objects such as fallen type.

**Ruler**—24″ thin metal, marked in inches and picas. Its thinness allows for accuracy while measuring.

**Brayers,** or rollers. Small wire-handled brayers for inking hard-to-reach areas; rubber roller width, from ¼″ to 2″. Large aluminum-handled brayer; rubber roller width, 6″ to 8″.

**Baren (Speedball)**—for handrubbing prints. The base is covered with a film of Teflon which slides easily over delicate papers and helps to prevent sheets from tearing during rubbing.

**Pressure Oilcan**—for dispensing solvents. One for benzine to clean type and cuts, another for a solvent such as Anchor R-228, Rubber Wash, to clean rollers.

**Sharpening Stone**—two-sided. A rough side for first grinding of cutting tools; a smooth side for polishing them. Use a few drops of oil on each side when sharpening.

(*Above*) Detail of print on white charcoal (Strathmore) paper. This is a single weight paper with a textured surface. Note that low spots in the paper do not make contact with the inked cut, creating a textured effect.

(*Below*) Example of a print on 80 lb. smooth-coated, glossy proofing stock (also available in mat finish). This paper produces a sharp line image.

# *Paper*

You can print on most kinds of paper. The choice will depend on what you plan to print and the printing method used. This choice should not be a casual one, since the look and feel of the finished print will be affected by the character of the paper—its thickness, color, finish, texture, and absorbency. You will find it rewarding to experiment with the different papers—not only because this is an exciting part of the printing process but also because you will learn how different papers receive ink differently and the various effects that can be achieved. Japanese printing papers are made from vegetable fibers which create high and low areas in the paper—that is, more ink will be concentrated on the fibers than between them. Keep in mind that any sizing or coating on the paper's surface reduces its absorbency and therefore its receptivity to ink.

The quality of the paper is another consideration. Paper made from woodpulp, called newsprint, is a cheap, low-quality paper very useful for proofing, whereas paper with a rag content is of fine quality. Ordinarily, bond paper is used for most business stationery, but an Aqua text paper might make a really distinctive letterhead. Printed material that will be handled often, like a business card or a booklet cover, might be printed on a heavy stock. If a great deal of work has gone into the design of a blockprint, a long-lasting paper such as an acid-free art paper would be preferable.

Bond papers, index card stock, and similar papers can be bought at stationery stores. Many art supply stores sell Japanese and other printing papers by the sheet. Paper supply houses can advise you on special needs and will send, on request, bound booklets of paper samples. See suppliers list.

**Watermark.** Many manufacturers will indicate, by use of the watermark, what they consider the preferred side for printing—the one from which the watermark can be read. Most of the time the two sides of the paper have different textures, but often it is really a matter of preference which side you decide to use.

**Dampening.** In general most relief printing is done on dry papers, but if a paper should prove too stiff, dampening can be done by putting a few sheets of newsprint or blotting paper on a sheet of glass or metal, dampening the paper, and then laying one or two printing sheets on top. Continue to interlay papers in this manner for the amount wanted and weight them down with a further sheet of glass or metal. To dry, reverse the process by using dry papers in between the damp printing papers and applying weight. Japanese papers can be dampened if you want them to pick up more texture from the printing surface.

# *Inks*

Both oil- and water-based inks are used in printmaking. Letterpress inks, which are oil-based, are recommended for most methods described in this book; linoleum block inks can also be used. Those new to printmaking, however, should experiment with both oil and water inks to learn how they differ and how to use each effectively.

## OIL-BASED INK

Oil ink spreads more readily and produces a more vigorous color than water ink but requires a drying period after printing. If its consistency, which resembles toothpaste, is too thin, thicken it with a pinch of cornstarch; if too thick, thin it with a drop or two of benzine or light machine oil. Ink comes in tubes and cans. Tubes are easy to manage and can be kept for a long period without the ink drying out. Their color range is not as large, however, and they are the more expensive of the two. Commercial inkhouses carry a large variety of stock colors ready for shipping in 1 lb. cans. Once a can is opened and exposed to air, its surface will harden and in time form a crust which must be completely removed before using.

**Mixing.** With a palette knife, mix ink on a fairly thick glass slab. The slab should be large enough for spreading the ink with a brayer while still leaving room for mixing another color. Experiment with very small amounts and always begin with the lightest color.

**Inking.** A good consistency is indicated when the ink slowly drips from the palette knife. Roll out the ink thoroughly with a brayer so that it makes a slight hissing sound when applied to the printing surface.

## WATER-BASED INK

This ink gives a flat, dense appearance and does not roll out as well as oil ink. When thinned with water it will cover an area with a light wash, and because it dries so quickly is useful for overprinting. Clean-up is so easy—just water does it.

## SOLVENTS

Kerosene, gasoline, benzine, or painter's naphtha can be used. They can be applied with paper towels, rags or lint-free "wipes." Most rubber rollers and brayers can be cleaned with these solvents, but to prolong the life of the rubber, use Anchor-228 Rubberwash or equivalent. For gelatin rollers, use kerosene.

*Caution:* Solvents should be kept in closed cans, away from heat or flame. Use only in well-ventilated areas and wear rubber gloves to avoid direct contact with skin. *Follow all directions on containers.* Rags saturated with solvents may start a fire, so discard after using.

*(Above)* Dabbing ink on glass slab prior to rolling out ink.

*(Below)* Rolling out ink, using criss-cross strokes with a brayer.

Vegetables cut and inked for stamping.

Hand-rubbing with a Speedball baren.

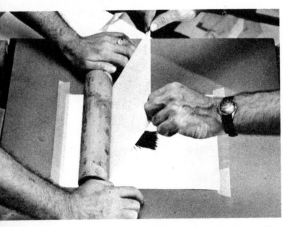

Rolling an inked feather between two sheets of paper.

# Hand-printing Techniques

Many of the objects that surround us have surfaces and shapes that can be printed. By inking the object and transferring its impression onto paper, textures and patterns of surprising beauty will be revealed, and you will come to discover the designs that exist in the most familiar materials.

Surfaces can be scratched with sandpaper, rasps, and wire brushes. Surfaces can also be built up by gluing on flat materials such as string, wood strips, fabric, or corrugated board—or simply use the glue itself, dribbled into a pattern and allowed to dry.

## STAMPING

Stamping is as simple as a fingerprint. Any object that will accept ink, has a smooth surface, and is convenient to handle can be transferred to paper to make an impression. Very often the stamped design is created by the object itself—such as an onion, a piece of wood or a sponge. The object can be inked with a brayer, or with a brush, or simply dipped into ink that has been rolled out on a glass slab. By carving into the object, however, you will have made a relief stamp. This stamp can be used for a series of repeat designs, or for overlaying of impressions in different colors. Anything that can be cut into will hold a design. For this technique see pages 36–37.

## RUBBING

Making a rubbing is one of the most direct and creative ways to print. It enables you to vary the amount of pressure throughout the printing area. Through this method tonal effects can be controlled and the very character of the print altered. Experiment freely with objects around you. Notice if they have textures or patterns—such as those of embossed designs, cardboard, ridged wallpapers, or straw matting. Apply ink to them with a brayer, press paper on, and rub with a flat wooden spoon. The precise quality and texture of the object will be revealed by this process. For this technique see pages 38–39.

## ROLLING

In this method a clear print impression can be made, particularly from fine detailed objects such as a leaf, a fern, a feather, or a sprig. There are two interesting features to this technique. One is that details, even though very fine, will print clearly and will take on additional meaning in terms of the design pattern. The other is that two impressions can be made simultaneously by inking both sides of the object, placing it between two sheets of paper, and applying pressure with a rolling pin. The double impression (front & back) affords a selection for choosing the final print. These impressions can be used effectively as art in greeting cards, posters, and announcements. For this technique see pages 40–41.

## OFFSETTING

This term applies to any printing surface whose image is not directly impressed onto a surface. Instead it is transferred to an uninked brayer and then transferred (or offset) from the brayer. After a surface is completely inked, an uninked brayer is carefully run over it, lifting the inked image onto itself. The image now on the brayer is rolled over a sheet of paper. However, it need not be offset onto paper—any surface that is not concave or convex will do, such as a cylindrical jar. The brayer can roll several more turns to give multi-impressions. For this technique see pages 42–43.

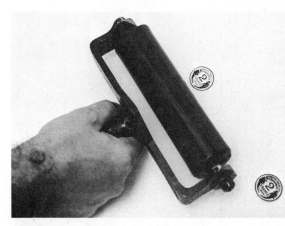

Offsetting an inked coin with an un-inked brayer.

## MASKING

With this technique, colors are masked out on a surface and by the use of shapes are overprinted and overlapped. The purpose is to prevent color from reaching certain areas on the paper. This is very simply done with torn or cut-out shapes of thin paper. These shapes combined with other shapes and different color backgrounds can make interesting and intricate designs. A surface is first inked with a solid color, then cut-out paper shapes are put over it to form any pattern desired. When a printing paper is placed over the surface and rubbed, the shapes will have become silhouettes of white against a background of color. This impression, when dry, can then be rubbed onto a wet-inked surface of a different color and with shapes in different positions. For this technique see pages 44–45.

Masking with paper shapes on an inked surface.

## ZINC CUTS

Anything that you have printed by the foregoing methods can become a permanent part of your collection of readily printable material. All that is required is to have its image transferred into a zinc cut. You can also have cuts made from line prints in old books, for use in printing pieces. Zinc cuts are printing plates onto which pictures, drawings, or type have been photographically transferred. A photoengraver will make a zinc cut for you and mount it on a base so that it will be ready for printing. Your hand print can also be reduced or enlarged to your specifications by this process. With a zinc cut you will be able to enhance any of your printed pieces with your own designs. For this technique see page 46.

Zinc cuts used for printed piece.

# *Linocuts*

Linoleum is in all ways very satisfying to work with; it cuts easily in any direction and is a splendid medium for color. It responds more readily than wood to cutting and is able to maintain fairly fine lines without crumbling. Linoleum is resilient and remarkably durable. Many impressions can be made from one linocut, and the last print remains as sharp as the first. This material is ideal for the beginner, and for children in art classes, yet it is also the means chosen by such artists as Matisse and Picasso to produce major works of art. Its surface textures range from smooth to a lightly stippled or burlap-like grain. Such textures can be maintained in the print with a light inking and can prove quite interesting. When more ink is applied to the cut and sufficient pressure exerted in the printing, these textures will usually disappear.

The linoleum used most often in printmaking is ⅛″ Battleship. This and other linoleum is to be found in most floor covering stores. You can buy linoleum by the yard, but leftover trimmings are much cheaper.

If cold weather has stiffened the linoleum, or if it will not lie flat and is awkward to handle, heating will make it softer and more pliable. Place it near a radiator, in the sun, or in a 300° oven for about ten minutes, with the door slightly open. When linoleum is almost too hot to handle, it cuts like butter.

**Readymade linoblocks** (white-coated linoleum usually mounted on plywood) can be bought at art supply stores. They are cut to specified sizes and will do the job if you can use the sizes and if only occasional use is required. However, if you want a different size, or want a quantity of linoblocks, it is easier and less expensive to make them yourself.

## PREPARING YOUR OWN LINOBLOCK

Compressed wood (such as Novoply), ¾″ thick, can be cut at a lumberyard to the size you want. This wood makes a firm base for linocuts and is free from the air pockets sometimes present in plywood. To cut the linoleum to size, place the wood on the linoleum surface and score around it with a mat knife. Then bend the linoleum back on the scored lines and slice through the burlap backing with the knife.

For permanent mounting, spread linoleum paste on the base with a toothed applicator (paste and applicator are available at hardware

linoleum cutters

V-shape

U-shape

Linocut and tools, with print of the cut as used in a booklet.

*(Facing page)* "Dragon Kite," 14″ x 16½″, by Erwin Schachner. Linocut.

Linocut and print of bird figure by Joseph Low. Whenever an inked cut is impressed directly on paper, it will print mirror-image.

Linoleum block is easily turned on Lazy Susan base for cutting. All areas not to print are cut away from the block. The hand holding the block is kept behind the gouge, for safety.

stores). Lay the cut linoleum on the base, matching all edges, roll it flat with a rolling pin, and allow it to dry overnight.

If, however, you plan to save your linocuts, the plywood bases will eventually confront you with a storage problem. In that case, use tape with adhesive on both sides to mount the linoleum. The cuts can then be easily removed and stacked for storing, and the base can be used again.

To complete the preparation of the block, spray the surface with flat white paint. Spray paint is preferable since brushmarks may show up in the finished print.

## PLACING THE DESIGN ON THE BLOCK

Designs drawn directly on linoblocks will be mirror-image when printed. If you want the design to appear as drawn, it must be reversed. To reverse a design, you can do any of the following:

1. *Draw the design on tracing paper and turn it face down on the block,* taping it in place with masking tape. Place a carbon, face down, under the tracing. Redraw the design, which will be visible through the back of the tracing paper, with a pencil or a stylus.

2. *Draw the design with a soft pencil (5B).* Turn the drawing face down on the block and rub it with a burnishing tool. To make the block more receptive to pencil graphite, you can heat the block in a 300° oven for ten minutes with the door slightly open. *Do not overheat* or you will damage its painted surface.

3. *Paint the design with graphite.* To do this, shave a soft graphite stick (6B) with a metal file until it turns to powder. When this is mixed with rubber cement thinner, it turns to a liquid and can be applied with a brush to tracing paper, which is then turned face down and rubbed. *Note:* Thinner must be added frequently since the liquid quickly evaporates.

"Fix" the transferred tracing to avoid wiping off or smearing the graphite while the block is being cut. A quick-drying clear plastic spray (Krylon Crystal Clear) should be used. This coating will also protect the surface of the block when it is cleaned with benzine after printing.

## TURNING THE BLOCK AS YOU CUT

The natural motion of the hand in using a gouging tool is forward and away from your body. To cut a small block, place it on the worktable and turn it as you work into the natural direction of the cutting tool. For large blocks (I have cut sizes as large as 24″ × 36″), it may become impossible to turn the block if it rests directly on the worktable. In order not to sacrifice the spontaneity and freedom of the engraved line when working on a large block, I have made a simple device which I call the Lazy Susan base and which turns a heavy block at the touch of a finger. This base is placed on the worktable with the casters up and the linoblock directly on them.

> **To Make A Lazy-Susan Base.** Cut a ¾″ board of Novoply or plywood to about two thirds of the length and width of the largest linoblock you plan to use. Buy a number of ball-bearing casters—the ones used on furniture legs—from a hardware store. The number you buy will depend on the size of your board. This caster is a chrome ball, which turns on ball bearings and is set into a cup that has a nail extending from its base. Attach the casters to the Novoply board about 4″ apart by drilling holes in the board and inserting the nails of the casters into the holes.

(*Above*) Tissue taped over block for checking progress during cutting.

## CUTTING

The most important safety rule for using gouges is that the free hand—the one *not* holding the gouge—is always *behind* the cutter. Start cutting by using the largest gouge to cut away the biggest areas, and end with a smaller tool to make the fine lines and details. Always cut under control so that you can stop the gouge at any time. Keep in mind that gouges slip easily and that once you have cut away or cut into an area to be printed, you will no longer have the design you planned. You will either have to start again with a fresh linoblock or improvise by changing the design to include the error. Do not cut all the way down to the burlap or even expose it. Leave a thin layer of linoleum everywhere. This keeps the linocut in one piece and prevents any burlap fibers from affecting the printing.

(*Below*) Graphite stick (6B) produces image of work in progress.

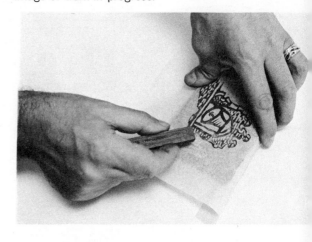

A scraper is used at the end to clean off any remaining high areas that should not be printed. It can also be used after pulling the first proof to clean off unwanted marks.

## PROOFING WITHOUT INK

As with other relief images described in this book, check your progress by taping soft tissue paper over the areas you want to examine, and rub with a 6B graphite stick. This technique is shown in the photos at right. Hold the side with the rubbing against a light to see how the finish will look.

Japanese woodcut of print on facing page.

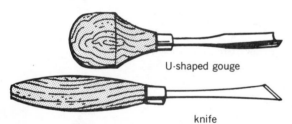

U-shaped gouge

knife

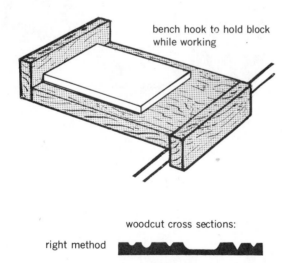

bench hook to hold block while working

woodcut cross sections:

right method

wrong method

# Woodcuts

A variety of woods are suitable for printmaking. Your choice will depend on preference and the work at hand—whether you want surface texture to be the essential element in the print, or whether you want to do detailed cutting. Warped wood can produce a beautiful handrubbed print. Texture can also be obtained from woods with strong natural grains, with knotholes, and from those that are weathered. For detailed work, the wood should be smooth and of a consistent thickness. It should be kiln-dried so that it will not crumble or split when worked. Hardwoods, such as pear and cherry, hold fine line incisions beautifully without splintering. They require very sharp tools and firm hand-cutting pressure. Softwoods, such as pine and plywood, are more easily cut and gouged, but care must be taken when cutting against the grain. Obtain these woods at lumberyards or art supply stores.

**Transferring a Design.** Simple designs can be drawn directly on the block. More complex designs are drawn on tracing paper with a soft 5B pencil. Transfer the design by placing it face down on the block and rubbing the back of the paper with a burnishing tool. Masking tape holds the paper in place. The transferred design is fixed with "workable spray fixative" to prevent it from being smeared when the block is cut. The block is then coated with a light brown wash of India ink mixed with water. This provides contrast while cutting by showing what areas remain still to be cut away.

Another way to transfer a design is to paste the tracing paper face down on the block with water-soluble glue. The design is then cut through the paper into the block. Oil rubbed on the back of the paper makes the drawing easier to see. Paper and glue can be removed with a damp sponge. Use straight knives here rather than gouges, which will rip the paper.

**Tools.** Gouges and knives are the basic tools. Gouges are V-shaped and U-shaped and vary from small ones that incise fine lines to large ones that carve deep furrows. The knife chosen should have a heavy-duty blade. Keep the tools sharpened by using a sharpening stone (see page 26). With the rough side of the stone, hone down the edge of the blade. With its smooth side remove burrs and polish the cutting edge.

**Cutting.** Usually the knife is used to cut around the contours of the design. Cut away from these areas according to the right method shown in the diagram (left), since any undercutting of raised areas will weaken them. Hold the knife like a pencil, and the gouge downward with its handle in your palm. The stroke is away from your body.

Hand-rubbed print from Japanese woodcut. Collection of Alexander Ross.

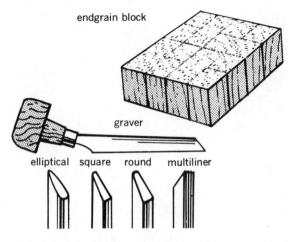

Gravers for wood engraving. Each category is made in a number of sizes which create thicker or thinner lines.

*(Above).* Set-up for engraving. Note print of finished engraving in background.

# Wood Engraving

Whereas the surface of woodcut blocks runs with the grain, the wood for engraving is upended and engraving is done on the crosscut surface. This crosscutting results in little or no visible grain and gives tremendous strength to the block, enabling it to be engraved many times in any direction with extremely fine lines, and to withstand a great many impressions. South American boxwood, used for engraving, has a very tight endgrain and great endurance. Maple can also be engraved, but will not hold as fine a line. An endgrain block has a smoothly sanded surface and consists of pieces of wood glued together. It is made to the height of type so that they can print together. It is advisable to print engravings on the proof or platen press.

**Transferring the Drawing.** For a reverse tracing, stain the block with black India ink and water. Or cover lightly with black letterpress ink, using a brayer. When the block is thoroughly dry, carbon paper, cut to block size, is put on, then the tracing paper with drawing side down; the latter is fastened with tape. Rub with a burnishing tool—not too hard or marks will appear on the print. Fix the design with a light coating of workable fixative; then with gravers cut the design on the block.

**Tools.** Three basic tools are needed: an elliptical graver, a round scorper, and a square scorper. Other tools are multiple liners which cut from two to a dozen lines at a single stroke. Since most cutting edges taper, line thicknesses are established by the depth of the cut. Cuts 1/32" deep are adequate for most work. Cut deeper around the outside edges of the block to avoid picking up unwanted ink when printing. An engraving tool is held with the ball end cupped in the palm and the thumb resting on the block as a pivot. Cutting pressure is applied by the palm. Tools must be surgically sharp to perform at their best, or they will make coarse lines in the wood. In addition to the tools mentioned, a *magnifying glass* is a necessity for seeing the hairline cuts while engraving. You will also need an *engraving pad*—a heavy leather-covered round pad. The engraving block is placed on it and turned in the natural direction of the tool. As regards *paper,* Basingwerk, light buff in color, makes for very good prints. Heavy Rives paper has a slight texture but, when dampened, produces beautiful impressions giving a slightly embossed look (see Dampening, page 16).

*(Left)* Sharpening a graver. It is held by an adjustable graver and burin sharpener for exact cutting angle. The point is run over the oiled sharpening stone in a circular motion.

"Le Cirque de l'Etoile Filant," by Georges Rouault. Wood engraving. Collection of the Museum of Modern Art, New York. Gift of the artist.

# *Type*

Type, another basic material that receives ink and causes an impression upon contact with paper, can be used for design effects as well as for conveying ideas. A single piece of foundry, or handset, type is a cast metal body bearing a letter, number, punctuation mark, etc. (all called "characters") in high relief on its printing surface. Its height—"type high"—is .918″. When a cut is combined with type (creating a "form"), it also must be type high.

Certain units of measurement are used to designate type size and type areas so that, when setting type, the number of words for any length of line can be determined accurately. The units are:

**Point**—measures type sizes. 1 point = 1/72″.
There are approximately 72 points in an inch.
**Pica**—measures type areas. 1 pica = 12 points.
There are approximately 6 picas in an inch.

For example, this line you are now reading is set to 25 pica width in 10 point Times Roman type style. A point indicates the size of the metal body and not necessarily the size of the typeface. When ordering type, be guided by the printed letter in the type catalog and by the sizes mentioned. It might be advisable to get a line gauge. This is marked in inches and picas, with a lip to hook over the edge of type for measuring line depth and height.

## HOW TO BUY TYPE

**Fonts.** Type is usually sold in fonts. A font contains an assortment of characters in one size and style, based on their frequency of occurrence in the English language, so that there will be more e's than q's, for example. Since each font may not have all the characters you require, be sure to check its listed contents. Standard

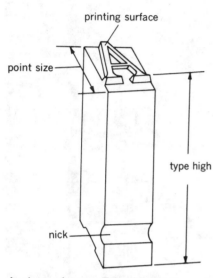

A piece of type. Type is always cast in mirror-image, so that it will read the right way when printed.

*(diagram labels: printing surface, point size, type high, nick)*

**California Job Case.** This case is divided into 89 compartments, each holding a specific type character or spacing material. The case is a shallow wooden drawer, approximately 32″ x 16″ x 1¼″. Several of the drawers are kept in a case rack, or type cabinet. The arrangement of type in the case is called the "lay of the case."

catalog abbreviations are:

cap.—capital letters      s.c.—small capital letters

l.c.—lower case or small letters      fig.—numerals

After purchasing a font, ink it and pull a proof (a trial print) to check for defective letters. The type is then "broken up" and each character is placed into its assigned compartment in a type case.

**Type by the Word or Line.** If you want only a few words of type, or a line, you can buy either individual characters or type set on a slug and cast in one piece.

**Transfer Type.** These are single characters on paper sheets, sold at art supply stores. They can be easily transferred onto paper in any position by rubbing. A zinc cut can then be made of the word or line.

## TYPE STYLES

One of the first concerns of a printmaker when using type is the selection of the typeface or style. The majority of the typefaces in common use, all supplied in a variety of sizes, belong to the following categories:

**Roman**—Letters with graduated serifs (the finishing line of a letter) and thick and thin strokes.

**Abstract** (or Sans Serif)—Letters having a square appearance and lines of uniform thickness.

**Cursive**—Letters slanting to the right, resembling handwriting.

**Decorative**—Letters with ornamental characteristics or individual design that place them outside the other categories.

In addition there are variations in the style of a particular typeface, such as Italics, Expanded, Condensed. Type also comes in Bold, Demi-bold and Light, which refers to the line weight of the type. Small Capitals, the same size as the letter x, are also available.

The tendency for the beginner is to use different faces together. However, until more experience is acquired, it is best to limit styles to the following suggestions:

**a.** Use the same face in different sizes and/or its variations.

**b.** For contrast, mix faces from two of the above categories.

## ORNAMENTS

Ornaments, borders, rules and ornate initial letters are illustrative type elements that are arranged to decorate a printed piece. Usually, they are not part of type fonts, but are purchased separately. Type catalogs are veritable treasure houses of these designs. Cast in the same manner as type and of the same height, they are available in either single units or in long solid lines, in mixed fonts, and in point sizes to fit with type. Lines, solid, dotted, and dashed, come in various widths and have to be cut to size. Borders must be cut to the length of lines or joined to make a full line.

Variety in type styles, used in combination with borders and decorations in an English circus bill of 1840.

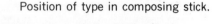

Position of type in composing stick.

Picking up type characters one at a time from the type case for arrangement in the composing stick.

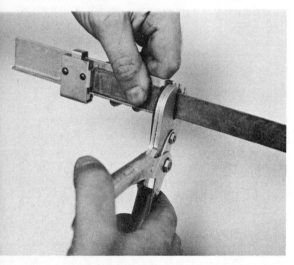

Cutting leading to size with a slug cutter.

_____

2 pt. lead

_____

6 pt. slug

# Type Setting

It will be helpful to make a diagram of the arrangement of type in the type case and have it handy so that you will know from which compartment to pick up the type and to which to return it.

### ASSEMBLING TYPE IN COMPOSING STICK

Type is arranged in a small metal tray called a composing stick, which will hold several lines. Pick up the characters one at a time from the type case and place into the stick, as shown in the diagram on this page at upper left. Each piece of type has a nick on one side which is easily felt with the fingers, so that you will know without looking whether it is in the correct position.

**Composing Sticks** are available in various sizes. Their given sizes, however, indicate dimensions and not the length of line that can be set. Some space is taken up by the "knee," a movable metal bracket which adjusts to the length of line desired.

### SPACES

After the type has been arranged, spacing is inserted so that the type will fit tightly and firmly in one position without wobbling from side to side. Do not force in more spacing than is necessary. Spaces consist of less than type high non-printing metal bodies. With each type size you buy, you will need a font of spaces. They come in several widths and are used wherever spaces are to occur, such as between words, at the beginning and end of paragraphs, and in centering a heading. Thin spaces, or hair spaces, are made of copper or brass but can be cut from index cards or other stiff paper.

### LEADING

After a line is set, leading is put in by means of "leads" or "slugs." Each line of type should have leading inserted above and below. Whether you use leads or slugs depends upon the spacing you want. A standard lead is 2 pts. thick and a slug 6 pts. (or ½ a pica). They can be purchased from suppliers in strips that you cut to size with a slug cutter (metal shears). This has an adjustable pica rule for cutting the leading at right angles and to the exact length of a line of type. Leading, like all spacing material, is less than type high and will not print.

### TRANSFERRING TYPE

When the stick is full, release the bracket and carefully slide the type to an imposing stone. If a chase—a cast-iron frame—is used, as on the platen press, place the type inside it on the stone. Press the leading together, while transferring, and hold the sides to prevent type from falling apart. Cellophane tape, or string, or "magnet locks" can be used to help keep type together.

**Imposing Stone** simply refers to any smooth and level surface on which type and/or cuts are assembled. On the proof press, the bed plate in the press can become the imposing stone. If the press is in use, a galley, which is a metal tray, can be used. Type can be left on the galley when printing on the proof press provided the bed plate, which is the same thickness as the galley, is removed. Type can also be stored on the galley before being returned to the type case. When using the platen press, a smooth piece of marble, or a steel plate, can serve as the stone.

## LOCKING UP

The type or form (type and cuts combined) is now ready to be locked up so that it will not move during printing.

**Furniture,** made of metal or wood, is used to fill in the large areas of open spaces around type and between paragraphs. The metal is shaped to size in square and rectangular pieces. The wood is cut to the lengths needed with a coping saw.

**Quoins,** metal wedges or rectangular-shapes, separate furniture from leading on presses. Midget quoins are adequate for table model platen presses. Usually only one quoin is needed on the short side of the form and two on the long side. They take up any slack left by the spacing material and apply pressure against type to hold it straight. Pressure is applied gradually and evenly with a quoin key which tightens the horizontal and vertical lineup. Tighten the quoins but just a little, since type has to be planed before the form is completely locked up.

**Planing.** In using many small pieces of type, you must be sure that none are sticking up or they will punch through the paper and also prevent other type from printing. A smooth flat block of wood, a planer, is used to level type in a form. Lay the planer flat over the face of the form and tap lightly with a small hammer or quoin key. Once type is planed, the quoins can be firmly tightened, but do this slowly, each quoin in turn, a little at a time, to prevent the type from buckling. What is to be avoided here is locking up one side completely before the other sides have been tightened.

**Magnet Locks** are used to hold type in place on the proof press. They are placed on all four sides of the type form, directly on the steel bed of the press, and are pushed tightly against the form for lock-up. A magnet lock is removed from the press bed by placing another magnet lock on it, attracting poles down, and twisting.

All that is left is to ink and print. After printing, clean the type with benzine or a type wash and return type to the type case.

Materials used in lock-up:
1 Font
2 Wood furniture
3 Metal furniture
4 Quoin and key

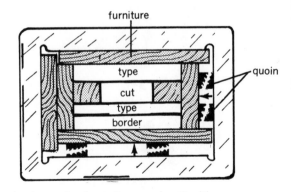

Lock-up of a form (type and cut) with furniture and quoins.

# Printing in Two or More Colors

Multicolor printing may be done in several ways and some approaches to it are described here. Traditionally, if the colors are to overlap, the lighter ones are printed first and the darker ones last. For the purposes of printmaking, black is considered a color.

**One Cut for Several Impressions.** A multicolor print can be made by printing with one cut separately in different colors and positions to give the effect of animation or provide a fuller illustration. For example, a group can be suggested by cutting an image on a block and printing it in one color; a different color is then applied to the block. Printing continues by changing position and color of the same cut.

**One Cut for Two or More Colors.** More than one color can be inked on a single block provided the color areas do not overlap or do not butt. The register board and the proof press work well with this method, permitting the application of a number of colors, with small brayers, before the ink dries.

**Separate Cuts for Adjoining or Overlapping Colors.** In this method, each color in the design is usually cut on a separate block, and each color is printed as a separate step. This method, called color registration, allows each color to fall exactly in the correct position on the sheet. For this to be done, every block to be printed must maintain the same position in relation to the printing paper. Two impressions can be spoiled by a third, if it is printed "off-register". See Register board, page 34, for further details.

The following method is a departure from the usual procedure of cutting a separate block for each overlapping color. Parts of a single linoblock are cut away after each impression until finally only the smallest area is left with which to print the last color. Before cutting the linoblock it can be used to print a background color; then cut any shapes away or make any lines that you want. The block is re-inked and printed, in register, over the first color. Continue to remove more lino from the block after each impression. Each new color is printed over the previous ones. This method was used by Picasso in making the linocut prints shown on pages 9 and 63.

**Hand-coloring the Keyblock.** In this method, after the design is printed, color is applied with brushes to the front or back of the paper; when coloring the back, the absorbency of Japanese paper permits the color to bleed through to the other side. In this way soft edges of color are obtained. Each print is individually hand-colored.

*(Facing page)* "Struwelpeter," by Joseph Low. Linocut. An example of two-color printing. The orange color is designed to accent the key block.

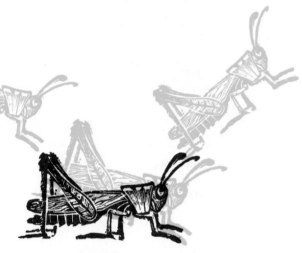

Repeating one cut for several impressions gives the effect of animation and creates a fuller illustration.

block **A**

block **B**

# Register Board

A simple demonstration of multicolor printing can be done with a register board that you can make yourself. The register board may be used to hold the paper and the block stationary, and in the correct position, while making a multicolor print. It can also be used to hold paper in place for a one-color print.

A separate block must be cut for each color planned. The relief design of the key block—the block used as guide for registering the others and usually the one with the darkest color—must be transferred to each block that will be cut.

Block **A** is printed first. The two colors are applied with separate brayers.

Block **B** is printed in black over the impression from block **A**. Lower section of block **B** is registered to meet the bottom of the figure of block **A**. The other register point is the devil's nostrils.

"Trials of Job," 15" x 22¼", by Erwin Schachner. Linocut. An example of a three-color print made with two blocks.

Method for registering paper to block. The paper should be firmly clamped before it makes contact with the inked block.

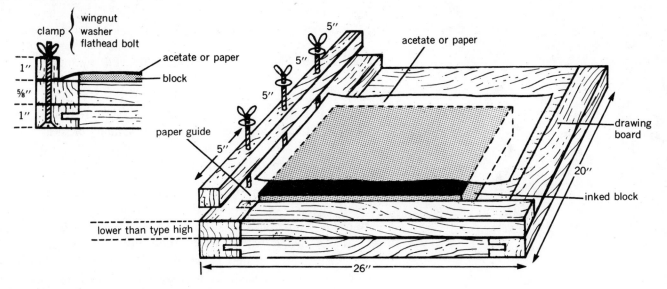

## TO PREPARE CUTS FOR REGISTRATION

1. Ink the key block with a letterpress dark ink and place it on the register board in the upper left corner.
2. Trim an .005″ sheet of clear acetate to the size of the printing sheet. Place it into the clamp and up to the bolts. Establish a fixed position as a guide for the paper edge.
3. Lower the clamp onto the acetate and tighten the wingnuts. Make an impression by rubbing the back of the acetate with a blunt instrument or burnishing tool.
4. Remove the key block and place an uncut one under the acetate.
5. Transfer the impression from the acetate to the uncut block by rubbing.

This procedure is repeated for each color. When the impressions on the blocks have dried, draw its color on each block, in the area that it will be applied. Then cut away on each block those areas that are *not* to print, leaving the drawn image raised.

## PRINTING THE CUTS

1. Place the cut to be printed in the upper left corner of the register board.
2. Ink the cut in the color it is to print.
3. Place the printing paper up to the bolts in the clamp, again using the fixed point for the paper edge.
4. Lower the paper over the block and make the impression by rubbing the back of the sheet, taking care not to tear it.
5. Repeat the above steps for each block to be printed. Allow time for the impression to dry before each new color is rubbed on.

Vegetables cut, inked and stamped to create design patterns.

# Printing Without a Press

Any material that is rigid enough to take or to make an impression can be used in printing without a press. Relief, or raised, images can be made by building up a surface, or by cutting into it.

## STAMPING

The stamped design can be created by a textured object that has been inked and then pressed to paper. Examples of such designs are shown on this page. A relief design can also be carved from an object, such as a potato or carrot.

The stamped designs on the facing page were made by potatoes that were cut in half. To make similar designs, printing paper is first taped to a board to keep it from sliding. A design is then carved out in the vegetable with a knife. Apply ink to the vegetable with a brayer and press against paper. If the vegetable should contain water, it will have a tendency to resist the oil-based ink. In that case use a water ink or India ink, applied with a brush, for a blacker impression. Posterboard paint, which has a water base, can also be used and applied in various colors to make designs.

A stamp can also be made by drawing a design on a piece of cardboard, no less than ⅛″ thick. With a sharp straight knife cut around the outlines of the design and peel off the top layer of cardboard in those areas you do not want to print. Tape the cardboard to a block of wood. Ink the design and stamp against the paper.

Assorted objects that can be printed to create designs:

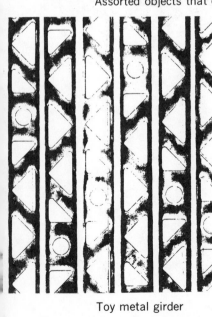

Toy metal girder

Plastic toy

Rolled corrugated board

Examples of potatoes cut in three different designs and of their use in printed pieces.

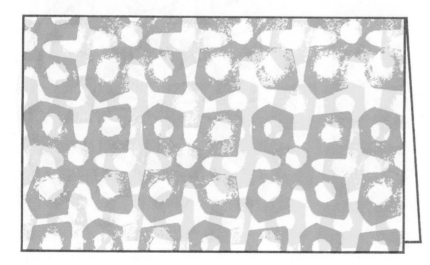

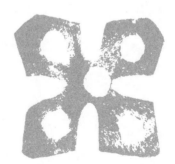

## RUBBING

Designs and textures can be impressed in a simple and direct manner by inking the object with a brayer, placing paper on it, and applying pressure to the back of the paper with a flat wooden spoon. Start rubbing from the center and work out towards the edges. Objects such as those shown on this and the facing page can successfully be made into print designs. This method also works well for woodcuts and linocuts of fairly large size.

Japanese papers are recommended for rubbing hard surfaces. They absorb the oil from the ink, leaving a clear concentration of pigment on the paper surface. Traces of oil will appear on the back of the sheet during rubbing and will give you an indication of how well the print is taking. In this way you can see where to vary pressure to create different tones. Papers such as Hosho, Moriki, Okawara, Troya, and Shogun, which have the feel of facial tissues, are best for hand rubbing.

To a certain extent, most papers will adhere to a heavily inked surface but care should be taken not to let the paper shift while rubbing. A sheet of thin paper is placed between the rubbing tool and the printing paper for protection against tool markings or tears while rubbing. A register board (see page 34) can be used to hold the printing paper in place. A soft cloth or pad, pushed into the lower areas of the surface, will pick up ink from a variety of depths.

Rubbing with a Japanese wooden paddle to obtain a print.

*(Below)* String, strawmat, corrugated board, and crumpled foil create a variety of textures. *(Right)* Impression rubbed from the base of a cut-glass platter.

Three impressions made from embossed vinyl wall coverings.

Objects embedded in plasticene create relief impressions *(above)* and silhouette design *(below)*.

Making a double print of a feather.

*(Above)* Inked feather is carefully placed between two sheets of paper.

*(Below)* One pass with a rolling pin over the top sheet creates two impressions.

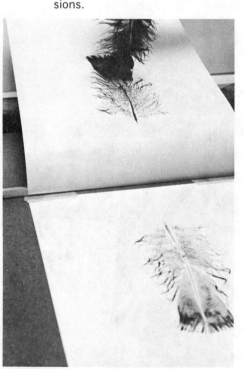

## ROLLING

Through the method of hand rolling, clean print impressions can be made of objects that have fine details or that are delicate and fragile. The effectiveness of this technique is illustrated in the finished prints shown below. The feather was inked on front and on back and then placed between two sheets of printing paper. A rolling pin applied the pressure for making the double impression—prints of both sides. By this process, details in the object become pronounced and clear and can reveal unexpected qualities. No two sets of prints are identical. All impressions will be the same size as the object but if a zinc cut is made (see page 46), the print can be altered according to the size desired. These impressions can then be incorporated as art for printing pieces such as greeting cards, posters, and announcements.

In using the bulkier evergreen sprig (facing page), an added dimension was achieved since the lower inked areas were not able to meet the paper during rolling. This is an example of the value of experimenting with different objects.

Silhouettes are also easily created by placing a flat object, such as an uninked leaf, on a sheet of printing paper. An inked brayer is then rolled over the surface of paper and object, creating a silhouette where the ink did not make contact with the paper. Strips of paper or yarn wrapped around an inked brayer before rolling it on paper will also create interesting patterns.

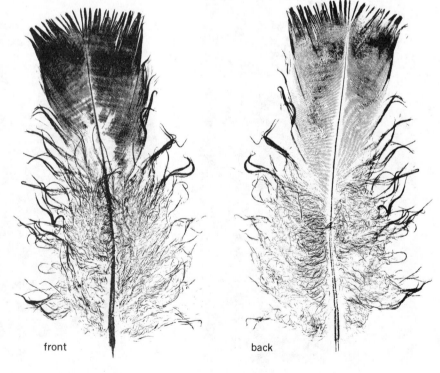

front                              back

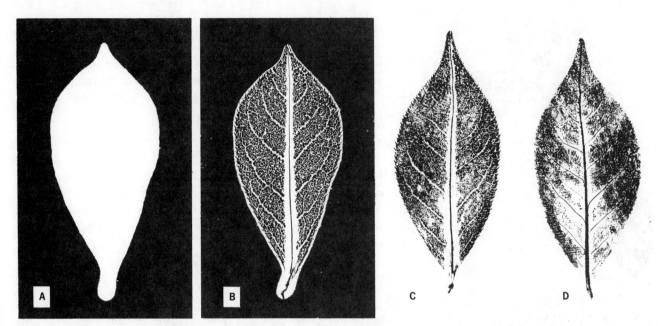

Sumac leaf printed for four different effects. **A** Inked brayer rolled over uninked leaf onto paper. **B** Inked leaf wrapped around inked brayer and rolled onto paper. **C** and **D** Inked leaf printed between two sheets of paper with a rolling pin.

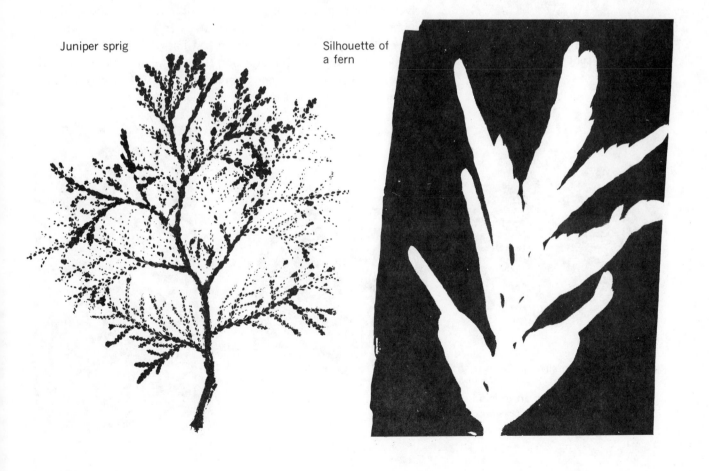

Juniper sprig

Silhouette of a fern

Offsetting can produce several impressions by continuous rolling of the brayer.

## OFFSETTING

This is a method of obtaining detailed or fine designs. Experimenting with embossed and textured surfaces may prove to be an exciting adventure and will be an invaluable exercise for the prints you want to make. This technique lends itself to creating repeats, patterns, and designs for large surfaces.

After completely inking the surface to be offset with a brayer, run an uninked brayer carefully over it. The inked impression will then be transferred to the brayer which in turn offsets it to the printing paper. The size of the printed image will depend upon the width and circumference of the brayer. This brayer must be completely clean and free from traces of other transfers. A smooth or glossy paper will pick up the most delicate details. An 80 lb. white coated stock is excellent to use for any offsetting designs you may wish to have made into a zinc cut.

Larger prints can be made by printing on two sheets, trimming and joining them. The brayer can be rolled several turns to give multi-impressions. If the object is too long for the brayer to pick up in one turn, the offset images will overlap. In that case, place the object at an angle to the brayer and obtain separate impressions (see trivet illustration on facing page). The darkest impression will be the first. Every time you make a new transfer, you have to start with a clean brayer. When the ink of the first impression is dry, it can be overprinted with a different color. Unlike some objects, such as feathers, which bear only one impression, hard surface objects made of metal, wood or iron can be offset indefinitely.

(Above) Mexican silver pin with (right) offset impression. (Far right) Wood fretwork printed from an Indian reading stand. Here two impressions have been joined at the middle.

*(Above)* By combining and adapting impressions or parts of impressions, borders and ornaments can be created for use in printing pieces such as greeting cards and announcements. Once your design is developed, it can be made into a zinc cut for printing on a press.

*(Left)* Inked trivet turned at an angle to an uninked brayer to prevent impression from overlapping when offsetting.

*(Below)* Part of an iron trivet with two repeat impressions assembled to create a decorative fish design.

Examples of masking technique, using two colors with two sets of paper cutouts. A third color is created through overprinting.

**A** Paper cutouts placed on yellow inked base, overlaid with a sheet of printing paper and hand-rubbed. The print is allowed to dry.

**B** A blue inked base is prepared with different paper cutout patterns.

**C** Finished print is achieved by overprinting the dried yellow impression onto the blue masked wet-inked block. Where the blue overprints the yellow, a third color, green, results. Overprinting for a third color is best achieved with transparent colored inks.

## MASKING

Designs and patterns can be easily created by masking out inked areas on a printing surface. A brayer is used to spread ink onto the entire surface; then cut-out or torn shapes of thin paper are placed on the surface. Other thin objects can be used, such as string, leaves, etc.

Cut a smooth-surfaced piece of wood or linoleum to the size of the print you want to make and then ink the surface with a brayer. Tear or cut various shapes out of a sheet of bond paper and place them on the inked surface to form the desired pattern. The printing sheet is then placed over this and pressure is applied by rubbing.

Interesting designs can be created when using transparent inks of different colors. For example, the first impression (after it has dried) can be overprinted with other colors and different paper cutouts. Also a deeper tone of the color is obtained by printing twice with the same ink. When the cutout pattern is changed for the second impression, you will get light and dark areas of color, together with lighter areas that were masked out by the cutout patterns. A register board or a proof press can be used for this technique.

Another way of masking to obtain a design is to cut shapes in a sheet of paper, then place the paper over the inked surface. Printing paper is placed over the mask and rubbed. This results in silhouette color shapes.

Placing paper cutouts on an inked block. When a sheet of paper is placed over this and rubbed, a print of the exposed black area will result.

# Zinc Cuts

Any hand print can be made into a zinc cut for use in a printing press. The zinc cut is made from the art to the size desired—through the process of photoengraving, its size can be reduced or enlarged.

Zinc cuts are printing plates onto which black and white lineprints, drawings, or type have been photographically transferred. The areas not to print are etched away, leaving a raised surface for inking, and the resulting cut is mounted onto a wooden base. The cut can be locked into position with type (see page 31), since the base has been squared off to the margins of the illustration.

When selecting art to be made into a zinc cut, make sure that it is on white, or near white, paper without colors or colored background. Light blue will drop out and will not reproduce, but red or deep orange will reproduce like black and show up on the finished cut. Since this is a photographic process, all defects or broken lines on the original print will reproduce exactly unless they are first corrected with black ink. Note that fine open spaces will fill in on extreme reductions.

The photoengraver will reproduce your print in a zinc cut to the size you specify. (See diagram below left for scaling.) Remember that as the width of the print increases or decreases, so will its height.

To order a cut:

**1.** Tape a sheet of tracing paper over the original print.

**2.** With a ruler, draw a line across the width or height of the original.

**3.** Indicate the desired size under the drawn line.

Photoengravers, when asked, will usually supply proofs of zinc cuts. The proofs can be printed on glassine paper and can be used in place of registration acetate for proofing (see step 3, page 74). If using cut and type together, by placing the glassine image over the type you will be able to visualize how the finished print will look.

Four zinc cuts used in making a two-color business card. The individual cuts were also used in other printings.

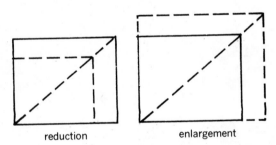

reduction          enlargement

Method for scaling a print to a reduced or enlarged size for a zinc cut.

*(Facing page)* Assemblage of assorted objects printed by hand stamping and offsetting techniques. Designs can be overlapped with different colors for a more exciting effect.

"Quill and Ink Vendor," 24" x 26", from the "Cryes of Londontown" series, by Erwin Schachner. Linocut. Two blocks were used, one for each color, on a colored stock.

## *Printing With a Press*

The primary purpose of a press is to transfer an image from a relief surface by mechanical pressure, allowing for the creation of a print in one motion and in larger quantity than would be possible by hand. In addition, mechanical pressure exerts sufficient force to permit the use of stiff papers which are impossible to print by hand, especially when the image has delicate details.

The proof press and the platen press described in this part of the book represent the basic models for presses used in relief printing. In the proof press—the simpler of the two—the paper is placed on an inked block, and a roller moves over it applying pressure in the manner of a rolling pin. The platen press works on the principle of the rubber stamp; the paper is pressed flat against the type form so that pressure is distributed evenly over the whole surface.

From these basic principles, a great many presses were designed by different manufacturers who invented labor-saving devices to solve specific problems, and introduced innovations to provide for special uses. Your choice of a press will depend on such factors as expense, size of press, space available and labor-saving devices desired.

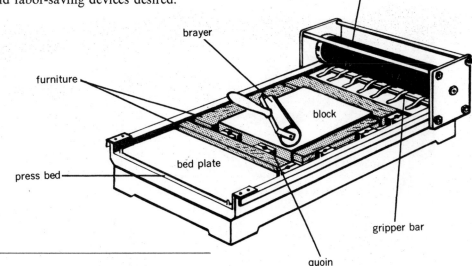

Proof press showing cut in lock-up

## *The Proof Press*

Like all techniques described in this book, the proof press prints from raised surfaces. It will accurately reproduce zinc cuts, small type, or the delicate details of wood engravings. Woodcuts can also be printed, but if an even print is desired the cuts must be on smoothly sanded wood, as perfectly level as possible. Such blocks are obtainable through dealers (see list of suppliers). If the wood is not level, surface irregularities will appear on the finished print.

Linoleum mounted on a level base will produce clean prints of large even-colored areas. Since the material is so resilient the pressure

applied against it by the impression roller will make up for most minor variations from type high. The roller is to the proof press what the rolling pin is to hand printing–it presses the paper onto the printing surface.

Materials such as cardboard, scraps of paper, and string can also be printed when glued to a level board provided that none of them exceed type high, or a slight variation from type high, at any point. If they should, the roller will be stopped at that point, unable to move further. Avoid using hard or sharp materials since these may damage the roller.

The proof press has a generous-size printing area, and when equipped with a gripper bar to position the paper, can produce clean prints without a great deal of preparation. The basic model of this press is far less expensive, less complicated, and lighter in weight than most platen presses of comparable printing sizes. Proof presses can be bought new from the manufacturer but are also obtainable used from dealers or at auctions (see list of suppliers).

Somewhat more complex models have refinements and labor-saving devices that make the operations to be described here semi- or fully automatic. Most of these presses have a semi-automatic inking device, and a roller that can be raised or lowered to allow for the use of various thicknesses of paper. Complex and expensive equipment, however, is not necessary to make quality prints; these can be made as well on the basic model so long as the preparation procedure is carefully followed.

### HOW THE PRESS WORKS

The form (type and cuts) is placed onto the press and is inked with a brayer. The printing paper is positioned on the form, and the impression roller, which is on steel rails, moves over the back of the paper once. The print is then peeled from the form and hung up to dry.

### PAPER

Smooth-surfaced papers work best on a proof press. They make better overall contact with the inked form and produce cleaner, more even prints than do textured papers. Interesting effects can be obtained with textured papers, however, and their use should not be overlooked.

*(Facing page)* Assorted textures achieved from soft objects that have been cemented to a linoleum sheet and made type high for printing on the proof press. These suggest the interest that textures can create when used in part with cuts or type. Crumpled paper, sandpaper, yarn, wall coverings, and straw mat were some of the objects used.

Profile views of printing on proof press:

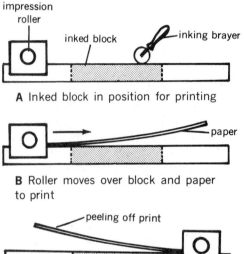

**A** Inked block in position for printing

**B** Roller moves over block and paper to print

**C** Print peeled from block

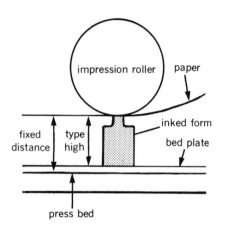

Every set-up on the proof press must be arranged within the fixed distance available. Adjustments such as overlaying and underlaying take up any slack that may exist between printing paper and the roller.

Standard type high gauge. Metal block *(left)* measures height of a piece of type; open area *(right)* measures printing blocks.

## TYPE HIGH ADJUSTMENTS

Before placing the form on the press bed and locking it up for printing, certain type high considerations have to be met. Proof presses usually come equipped with a steel plate, .050″ thick, which fits into the bed of the press (type high plus .050″ equals "fixed distance"). This bed plate can be left in the press or removed from it.

**Bed Plate Removed from Press.** If the bed plate is removed, the space of .050″ now gained can be used for the following adjustments:

1. A galley, a metal tray which served as an imposing stone, has the same .050″ thickness. With the bed plate out of the press, the type and/or type high cuts which have been locked up in the galley do not have to be removed for printing. Place the galley, with the printing material on it, directly into the press bed. Proofing paper or any paper stock of equivalent thickness can be used for printing. (Proofing paper is about as thick as an index card.)

2. Built-up printing surfaces (such as glue, cardboard, collages, etc.), which may be slightly higher than type high, can be accommodated.

3. If the level of the paper has to be raised to meet the roller or if the pressure of the paper against the form has to be increased, "underlaying" or "overlaying" is done.

   a. **Underlaying.** Normally the proof press will print on papers with a thickness of about an 80 lb. coated proofing stock or its equivalent. However, with the bed plate removed, there will be space for printing on heavier sheets, even posterboard, as long as thicknesses do not exceed .050″. To accommodate the sheets, place a padding of newsprint or other paper *under* the form. The padding should be trimmed to the size of the form. Use as many sheets as necessary until the heavy printing paper cannot be pulled out as the roller moves over it. This method works well when the printing material is in one piece, such as a zinc cut, woodcut, or linocut.

   b. **Overlaying.** Some papers that appear smooth will show tiny fibers when seen under a magnifying glass. These fibers create high and low areas on the paper and prevent it from making total contact with the inked form. In some cases additional pressure can squeeze the fibers so that the low areas between them will receive the ink. To apply pressure, place a padding of newsprint or other paper *over* the printing sheet. With certain papers, even maximum pressure, which is not recommended,

*(Facing page)* "Heritage," by Erwin Schachner. Linocut. Two blocks printed in white and black on Gold Tea Chest paper. Textural interest is achieved by working the surface with standard gouges and hammering in nail holes for dotted effect.

FUTURE, (noun): "that period of time in which our affairs prosper, our friends are true, and our happiness is assured."

will not compress the fibers sufficiently, and a gray or weak print will result. One way to overcome this is explained below —"Inking the Form."

*Note:* If more than a few small type characters are used, it is neither advisable nor practical to underlay them. Type must stand firmly in a galley or on a bed plate in the press in order to print. When stood on paper sheets, it is bound to wobble. If you want to print from type on posterboard or a paper thicker than 80 lb., do the following: Set type directly on the press bed with the bed plate removed. Test the thickness of the printing paper by placing it on the type and moving the roller over it. If the roller does not touch the paper, or a weak print results, place as many sheets of padding *over* the paper as necessary for a good print. You will know that there is too much padding or that the paper is too thick if the roller does not move freely or stops altogether. Do not force the roller or you may damage it.

## LOCK-UP

This term, as it is used for the proof press, means placing type, cuts, or other materials to be printed in a fixed position into the press so that they do not wobble or move.

If the printing form consists of one piece, such as a woodcut, linocut, or zinc cut, magnet locks placed around all four sides will usually hold it firmly enough for most printing. Magnet locks will also enable you to lift a one-piece cut out of the press bed and then replace it. (For color registration, the roller must return to its starting point after making the impression. On its return trip, it will pick up any ink remaining on the form unless the form is lifted from the bed. More information on returning the roller to its starting point follows on page 58.) A good idea is to affix masking tape to the bed plate and alongside the magnet locks—in this way you will know if any part of the form has moved.

When printing from a number of individual type pieces or a combination of type and cuts, it is better to lock them up securely so that they do not move, wobble, or fall apart. This is done by using furniture and securing the entire form with Quickset quoins. Lock-ups in the proof press are illustrated in the photographs at right.

## INKING THE FORM

Once the printing material has been locked up in the press, it is ready to be inked. Smooth-surfaced papers require only a thin

*(Facing page)* "Definition #6, Future," by Erwin Schachner. Linocut. One block. Inked with two colors the block was overprinted on stenciled red areas.

Method for simple lock-up, showing block with furniture and quoins. Once the block is positioned, it will remain in place until the end of the print run.

Method for lock-up with magnet locks. Tape is placed to mark positions of exact alignment. This lock-up allows the block to be lifted out before returning the roller for the next print.

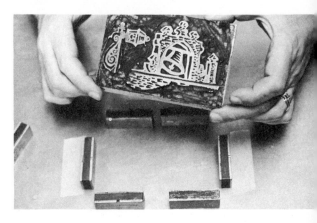

Inking the block with a brayer prior to making an impression.

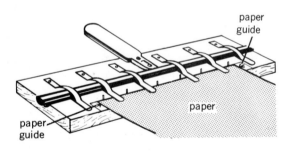

Gripper bar. It firmly and accurately holds the paper in place and establishes the position of paper to block.

layer of letterpress ink for a good impression. To ready the ink, place a small amount on a smooth glass slab and, with a clean brayer, roll it out with criss-crossed strokes, until you hear a hissing sound and the ink glistens like silk. Then, with the brayer, ink the form, using smooth, even strokes. Re-ink the brayer whenever necessary by rolling it over the glass slab. Keep in mind that the brayer will spread ink only in the size area corresponding to the dimension of its rubber roller. Continuous rolling of the brayer on the printing surface will result only in picking up part of the ink that you previously deposited.

When using certain papers whose fibers resist good ink coverage and produce a "gray" or weak print, roll out the ink on the glass slab as before, but not so thoroughly. Stop when it makes a crackling noise and its texture is that of gooseflesh. When this ink is applied to the form, the small bumps that it contains will flatten out in printing and fill in between the paper fibers and/or low spots on the textured papers. This is also the best way to apply a heavy layer of ink when an opaque color is used to overprint another color.

Remember to keep the ink capped when it is not in use or else a film will form over it. Protect the brayer when it is not in use by laying it on its supporting legs so that the rubber does not touch anything. This will prevent it from becoming flattened.

## POSITIONING THE PAPER

The paper is placed face down on the form with careful hand positioning. Type high wood can be placed next to the form and masking tape affixed from it to the paper to help maintain the paper in the proper position.

However, if you want to be sure of the exact size of all four margins on every paper to be printed, or wish to do multicolor printing, you will need a gripper bar to hold the paper in place such as the one made for the Nolan Standard Proof Presses.

## GRIPPER BAR

This bar locks into the press bed, under the roller and parallel to it. A lever opens and closes a number of steel clamps called grippers which hold each printing sheet in exactly the same position. This lever should be placed so that it extends beyond the open end of the press to permit free access for opening and closing the grippers. The grippers should be far enough forward so that paper can be inserted when the impression roller is rolled back to its farthest point. This gives access to the maximum area of the press bed.

(Facing page) "Cervantes," by Erwin Schachner. Woodcut. Printed on 1-ply Olive Fabriano imported paper.

CERVANTES

1547-
1616

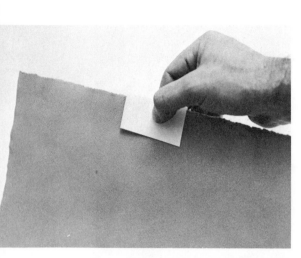

Paper fingers protect paper sheets during handling.

Hanging print to dry on a clothespin rack.

The gripper bar is lower than type high so that the impression roller can pass over it. When a sheet is slipped under the grippers as far as it will go, and the lever is closed, you have established the up and down position for all sheets cut to the same size—that is, the position where the printing surface will make contact on the paper. To fix the side to side position of the paper, place a small strip of masking tape as a guide on the gripper bar, butting the edge of the paper (diagram, page 56). All subsequent sheets will then be in the correct side to side position, when they are butting the tape.

### TO PRINT

If the gripper bar is being used, clamp the paper in correct position in the grippers, holding the loose end up so that it does not come into contact with the form. Move the impression roller once over the form, all the while allowing the paper to follow around the roller. This will prevent the paper from wrinkling. The impression is made, and the print is very carefully removed with "paper fingers" and hung up to dry.

**Paper Fingers** are recommended for handling the paper both before and after the impression is made in order to avoid fingerprints. They are easy to make from 1-ply Bristol paper or index card stock. Cut them to a convenient size and fold off-center so that there is an overlap of about ¼″. The printing paper can be easily scooped up with the extended edge, and if quite a number of these "fingers" are kept near the press, their use will soon become automatic.

**Drying Prints.** Two parallel lines, 20″ apart, made of rope, nylon cord, wire, or other material can be strung up to hang prints on for drying. The prints are hung perpendicular to the lines with clip-type clothespins that have holes drilled through them for the rope to pass through. Metal clamps with holes already in them can also be used, but they are more expensive.

**Returning the Impression Roller.** The roller is returned to its starting position. On its return trip, however, it must not pick up any ink remaining on the form. If magnet locks have been used to lock up the form, just lift the form from the press and return the roller. If type matter or a number of cuts and engravings are securely locked up with quoins, it is not advisable to unlock the form to lift it from the press. By placing a sheet of newsprint, or any other paper large enough to cover it, over the form, no ink will come in contact with the returning roller. The same sheet can be used a number of times, but be sure that the inked side never comes in contact with the roller since this can cause an impression on the back of your next printing sheet.

With the roller back in position, you can re-ink the form for the next print.

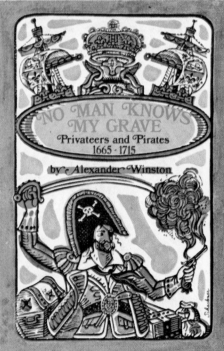

Print of black key block *(above)* and hand-colored print for use as book jacket *(right).* Here color was painted directly onto the print with watercolors and brushes.

Two prints, each 7″ x 9″, by Miriam Begg. *(Top)* "Tangled Web." Three colors (blue, brown, olive) on buff paper. *(Bottom)* "Tangled Web, Variation #1." Three colors (yellow, blue, red) on white paper.

These prints show how the use of different colors with the same blocks achieves different effects. By repositioning the plates, still other effects can be obtained.

## MULTICOLOR PRINTING AND COLOR REGISTRATION

Methods for creating all blocks necessary for multicolor printing and for establishing color registration in the actual printing are the same for the proof press as for the register board. Follow the directions on page 35. The main difference is that the paper is held by grippers instead of wingnuts.

For the actual printing, a clear impression of the key block on a sheet of .005″ acetate, cut to the exact size of the paper, will be necessary. If the sheet you have used for transferring the key design from one block to another has become smudged, remove the ink with benzine and make a new impression. Hang the acetate sheet to dry.

Place the dry acetate sheet printed side down into the grippers, which have remained in a fixed position with the side to side position established by masking tape. Each color block is then positioned in its turn directly under the acetate sheet and locked into place with magnets or quoins and furniture.

Remember, the first color is printed on all the sheets before the cut is removed. They are then hung to dry thoroughly before the next color is applied. When the cut for the second color is set into the press and inked, all sheets with the first color are rerun and are printed for the second color. Continue in this fashion until all colors have been printed. Each print must of course be thoroughly dry before the next color is printed.

"The Spanish Woman," 24⅝″ x 17⅜″, by Pablo Picasso, 1962. Linocut in three colors—light orange, deep brown, and black. Collection of the Museum of Modern Art, New York. Gift of the Saidenberg Gallery.

"Winter Moonlight," 12 11/16″ x 12¼″, by Ernst L. Kirchner, Woodcut, printed in color. Collection of the Museum of Modern Art, New York. Purchase Fund.

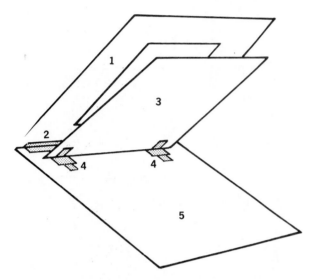

Method of matting print with paper hinges.

1 Mat with cutout window
2 Taped hinge
3 Print
4 Paper hinges (2-piece)
5 Mounting board

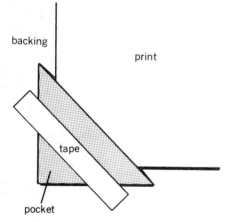

Method of placing print corners in paper pockets. A print so matted can be easily removed.

## CLEAN-UP

**The Impression Roller** is meant to roll smoothly, and therefore its sides, which are made of steel, should be kept clean and free from ink buildup or any other matter which could jam roller action. The top and underside of the rails should also be kept clean to allow for free movement of the ball bearings.

The rest of the roller is usually covered with smooth rubber. Be sure to take care of this surface. If the rubber should get holes or cuts in it or become damaged in any other way, the area of the damage will most likely not print. Avoid jamming the roller over the form and watch carefully for any type that might be sticking up. Keep ink, oil, kerosene, or any solution with an oil base away from the rubber.

**The Brayer** should be cleaned at the end of each day of use to protect it from the chemicals in the ink, which may cause the rubber to deteriorate.

*Note:* To clean both the rubber on the brayer and on the roller, use paper towels or wipes with Anchor R-228 Rubber Roller Wash, or any equivalent.

## EDITIONS

An edition is the number of prints that have been printed from the same blocks. The size of the edition is up to the printmaker. Each print is signed and numbered at the bottom, so that if there are twenty-five prints, they are numbered 1/25, 2/25, etc., to indicate that the prints are first and second in an edition of twenty-five. Always try to keep one perfect print for your own collection. If you should decide to print from the same blocks again, mark those prints "second edition" and change the colors in order to distinguish one edition from the other.

## MATTING YOUR PRINT

One reason for matting a print is protection, another is appearance. The print is placed between two mat boards, and a "window" for it is cut out of the top board. This is a good place to mention that a print is never trimmed. The mat boards are hinged together all along the top, on the inside, with paper hinging tape. The print is hinged to the back board with either Japanese paper hinges or stamp-mounting glassine hinges. To affix the hinges, use library paste or a homemade flour and water paste. Avoid using a synthetic adhesive, for in time it may discolor the print.

Instead of hinging the print, it can be slipped into corner pockets made from folded paper. This can be done only if the print has a wide border. The corner pockets can be affixed to the mat board with strips of paper tape. With this method, prints can be easily removed at any time.

Should you decide to frame your print, be certain that the glass is never in contact with it, for condensation of moisture can form inside the glass and harm the print.

## DISPLAYING YOUR PRINT

Where you decide to display your print is a matter of choice, but avoid hanging it where it receives direct sunlight. Also, since humidity can cause a print to deteriorate, be sure that it is hung on a dry wall.

"Still Life Under the Lamp," 21″ x 25¼″, by Pablo Picasso, 1962. Linocut. One block. From *Picasso Linocuts 1958–1963,* by Donald H. Karshan, Tudor Publishing Co. Collection of the Computer Applications Inc.

*(Above)* Detail of top section.

## An Example of Multicolor Printing and Color Registration

An intricate example of the techniques of overlapping colors and textures. Three blocks were used to achieve all the colors and printing was done on blue Japanese paper. A proof press was used. Sections of each block were inked in different colors with small brayers. Some transparent inks were used. Their colors change as they overprint other colors. Through overprinting, some colors also blend together, creating soft edges. White ink was used for contrast and to brighten over-printed colors and to achieve the stained glass effect.

*(Left)* Detail of heads.

*(Facing page)* "Madonna and Child," by Erwin Schachner. Linocut.

There was a king met a king
In a narrow lane;
Says this king to that king,
*Where have you been?*
O, I've been a-hunting
The buck and the doe.
*Pray lend me a dog
That I may do so.*
Take the dog greedy guts.
*What is his name?*
I've told you already.
*Pray tell me again.*
Greedy Guts! Greedy Guts!
Greedy Guts!

No need to repeat yourself when you call
Joseph Low in Newtown, Conn. Garden 6-2269

## *Platen Press*

The platen press inks and prints in one motion, which makes it ideal for fast printing of greeting cards, mailers, letterheads, etc. Once paper has been put on the platen—the flat smooth face of the press—and the form locked into the chase bed, the automatic inking and the easier paper feeding allow for a greater number of prints in less time than on the proof press. The preparation for printing takes somewhat longer, however, since pressure must be distributed evenly over the entire printing surface.

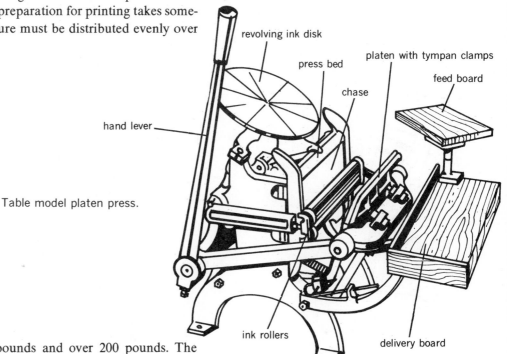

revolving ink disk

press bed

platen with tympan clamps

chase

feed board

hand lever

Table model platen press.

ink rollers

delivery board

**Table Models** weigh between 20 pounds and over 200 pounds. The size of the material you want to print should be a main factor in determining the press model you purchase. The smallest has the printing area of a business card and the largest about letterhead size. With some ingenuity, larger prints can be made by folding the paper stock in half and making an impression on both halves of the fold. Depending upon the size of the paper, it can be folded even more times to print a larger area.

**Motorized Floor Models** weigh a great deal more than the largest of the table models and provide greater areas for printing. It is possible to obtain a floor model in good working condition at an auction for a reasonably moderate price. A friend of mine did just that, paying the same price for a used floor model as I did for a new table model.

*(Facing page)* "Greedy Guts," designed, cut, and printed by Joseph Low (Eden Hill Press). A self-promotion piece printed on a Colt Armory Press. Printed in black and brown. Other colors were applied by hand with stencils cut in acetate.

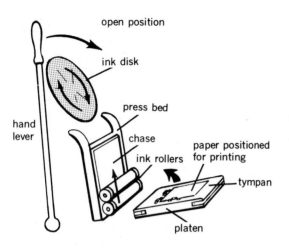

open position

ink disk

press bed

hand lever

chase

ink rollers

paper positioned for printing

tympan

platen

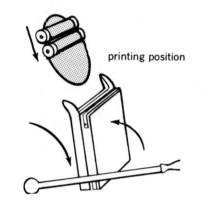

printing position

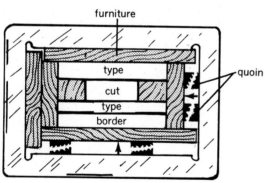

furniture

type

cut

type

border

quoin

Lock-up for chase. Pressure is exerted in two directions by quoins.

## PROCEDURE FOR PRINTING

Type and/or cuts are assembled on an imposing stone within the chase (a cast-iron frame) and are locked up for printing. The chase is then lifted and placed into the chase bed of the press, where it is secured by a spring hook or other locking device.

Table models are activated by a hand lever. Short downward pulls on this lever cause an ink disk to revolve and set rollers in motion distributing ink over the disk. When the lever is brought up, the rollers move down to ink the form. A sheet of printing paper is then placed on the platen. Printing takes place by pulling the lever all the way down; the rollers move up to the disk where they are re-inked as the press closes and the impression is made. When the lever is brought up, opening the press, the printed sheet is removed, and a new sheet is placed on the platen.

Floor models work on the same principle except that a motor activates a belt-driven flywheel so that opening and closing of the press is continuous and automatic. On some models, paper feeding and removal are also automatic.

## LOCK-UP

The inside measurements of the chase determine the maximum size of printing matter which can be set. Chase measurements are often used in printing catalogs when referring to press models. Keep in mind, however, that some of the space inside the chase is given up to leads, furniture, and quoins, thus reducing the actual area in which printing matter can be set.

Type and/or cuts are set up inside the chase on a surface serving as an imposing stone. Any smooth, hard surface will do, such as a marble slab or a steel plate. Place quoins on two adjacent sides of the form; the number of quoins will depend upon the size of the chase. Plane the type and gradually tighten the quoins, each in turn, with a quoin key, to assure a level printing surface. Do not lock up one side completely before the other sides have been tightened. (For more information on type setting and lock-up, see pages 30–31.)

Once the quoins are securely tightened, the chase can be lifted from the imposing stone, and the printing matter will not fall out. Place the chase into the bed of the press and secure it by a spring hook, or other fastening device, depending upon your press model.

## APPLYING THE INK

Wipe any dust or lint from the ink disk with a clean dry rag and check the ink rollers to be sure that they are clean. Put a few dabs of letterpress ink on the disk—the first impression will be a lightly inked

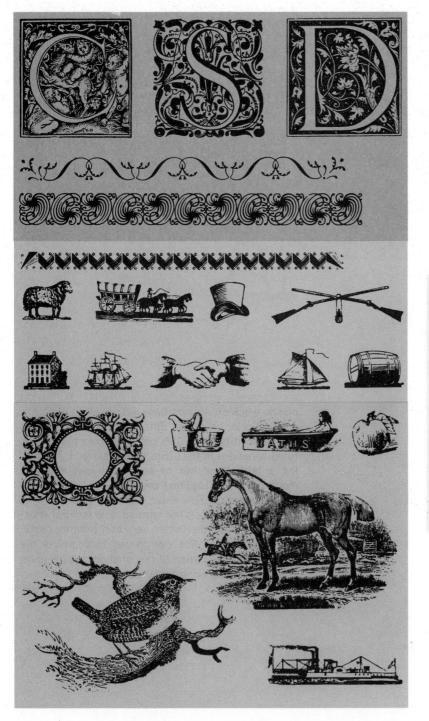

An example of combining line spots with type in a self-promotion piece.

Decorations such as these, available from library picture collections and books (subject to permission in the case of copyrighted material), can be transferred into zinc cuts. They can also be bought from a foundry (see suppliers list). Shown are decorated initials, various line "spots," and two wood engraving reproductions of Thomas Bewick's work.

"Little King with Clover"

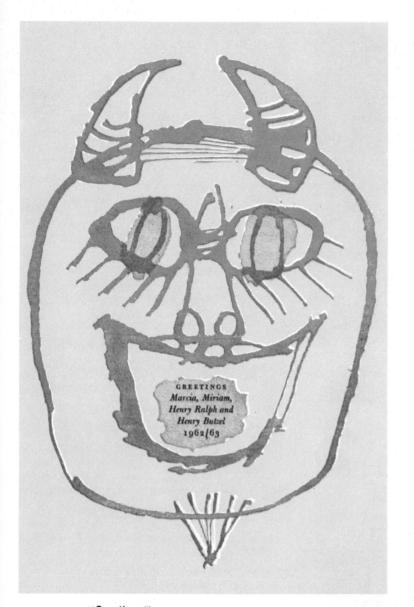

"Greetings"

### THREE PRINTS BY JOSEPH LOW.

All are linoleum cuts and achieve the effect of a spontaneous calligraphic line. "TiPi," a resilient plastic block on a wood base, was used to apply the areas of color. In "Dead Bird," the ochre was printed from a solid block of TiPi onto very thin paper. Textured variations in the ochre were achieved by spreading a fairly thick mix of acrylic polymer emulsion modeling paste (Liquitex) on a sheet of 2-ply Strathmore cardboard. This sheet was then placed behind the printing paper on the tympan. The textural effect is dependent on the use of very thin printing paper. The orange color was overprinted to complete the print. For an illustration of this method, see the lower diagram on the facing page.

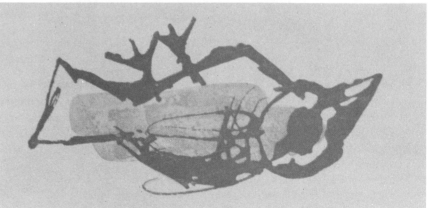

"Dead Bird"

one. Remember to recap the ink since it dries rapidly when exposed to air.

Short downward strokes on the hand lever will cause the ink disk to revolve and turn one notch with each pull, thereby spreading the ink as the rollers move over it. After the ink is well distributed on the disk, bring the lever all the way up so that the rollers can move down to ink the form. A fresh dab of ink should be placed on the disk for every ten or fifteen impressions, depending on the amount of ink that each sheet uses. Keep in mind that too much ink will result in a smudged or blurred print.

## POSITIONING THE PAPER

A sheet of hard-surfaced paper, called the tympan, is placed over the platen and bent into tympan clamps (see diagram, page 72). The purpose of this paper is to provide support for the printing paper. A sheet from a manila folder can be used as tympan paper.

Make a very lightly inked impression on the tympan. From this you will be able to tell exactly where the print will fall, and therefore where to position the paper. Make guide lines on the tympan to indicate the outside margins of the paper, or where you want the edges of the paper to be placed. Affix "gauge pins" along those guide lines—two pins on the bottom of the paper and one on the side. Gauge pins can be bought in various styles. These are usually positioned through small cuts in the tympan. Gauge pins can also be home-made from manila paper or index cards. Cut thin strips, raise a "bridge" in the center and paste the sides down onto the tympan. Be sure that all gauge pins are positioned on the tympan in places where they will not be crushed by furniture or quoins.

## PACKING THE TYMPAN

Before the paper is positioned, all the ink of the first impression is rubbed off the tympan with a rag so that no set-off impression will appear on the back of the printing paper. This is one reason why the first impression should be a light one.

Since the paper must make full contact with the form, in order to make a cleaner impression, smooth-surfaced paper stock rather than one of a heavy texture should be used. Stand the paper on the bottom gauge pins and move it over to meet the side pin. Add ink to the disk to the full strengh that you want to use, and pull a proof.

If the print is too light, you either do not have enough ink on the disk or the paper is not thick enough to meet the form. In the latter case insert one or more thin sheets of paper behind the tympan. This "packing" of the tympan (see diagram, page 72) increases the pres-

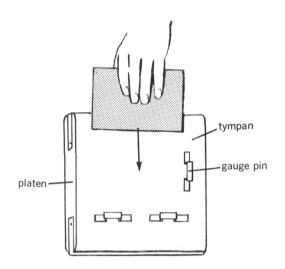

Homemade gauge pins are placed on the tympan sheet for positioning of paper or acetate sheet. Commercially made pins are called Spring Slide and Twin Grip.

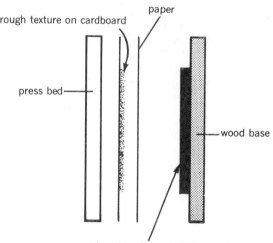

Method of obtaining a textural effect, using very thin paper between rough-textured cardboard and a resilient plastic block. (See "Dead Bird," facing page.)

sure that will be applied against the form, and will bring form and paper into closer contact.

Pack the tympan gradually until a sharp impression is made. Pressure should never be so excessive that the form is punching through to the back of the paper. This not only will result in a smudged impression but will eventually mar the type or cut.

The preferred amount of pressure is a "kiss" impression—one in which no indentation of type can be felt on the paper. At times, however, you might want a particular esthetic effect; in that case a slight indentation in the paper will add character to the print and will not damage type or cuts, especially in small runs.

### MAKE-READY

While proofing, you may notice that some portions of the form that should have received ink did not do so. Usually this means that there are low spots in the form, and the paper must be built up to meet them. This is done by overlaying and underlaying.

**Overlaying.** Cut pieces of thin tissue paper to the approximate shape and size of the poorly printed areas and paste them onto one of the packing sheets behind the tympan. Make-ready paste can be used, although sparingly, since paste has its own thickness. Rubber cement, another choice, will add less to the thickness of the overlay. Continue to build up the tissues until you are printing evenly, but add them gradually or else you might add one too many, and its shape will be visible on the print.

One way to determine where to position the overlays is by sticking a pin through the low spots in the tympan onto the packing sheet. Another way is to paste tissues directly onto a sheet on which an impression has been made. This sheet will clearly show where the low spots are, and if it is properly placed behind the tympan, the pasted tissues will be in the correct positions.

**Underlaying.** Cuts that have been made from linoleum or wood blocks may not be type high and will require building up. This is done by pasting underlays of cardboard or paper to the bottom of the block until type height is reached. A useful tool to determine type height is a Type High Gauge.

Minor adjustments sometimes can be made if one side of a cut is printing lighter than the others. Underlay the low side with cellophane tape, one strip at a time, until that section is high enough to make a clear impression.

### TO PRINT

As soon as you pull a proof that satisfies you, and there is enough

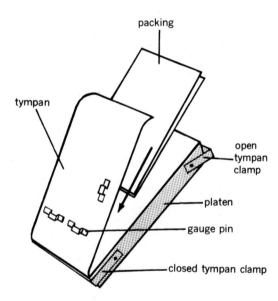

packing

tympan

open tympan clamp

platen

gauge pin

closed tympan clamp

Method of packing the tympan.

ink on the ink disk, stack sheets of printing paper onto the feed board and insert one into the gauge pins. Make your first print and place it face up on the delivery board. Do the same with subsequent prints. Be careful not to stack them too high or a set-off impression will appear on the backs. If set-off should occur, you can "slip sheet" the printing run—that is, after a print has been placed on the delivery board, place a sheet of paper between it and the next print.

## PRINTING IN TWO COLORS (Type, Zinc Cuts, and Wood Engravings)

These step-by-step instructions are for printing colors separately on the platen press, with neither color overlapping.

1. Set all printing matter for both colors into the chase, using leads, furniture, and quoins.
2. Remove, one at a time, all printing matter that you plan to print in the second color, and carefully refill those areas with spaces, and furniture.
3. Print the first color.
4. Clean the printing matter. Remove all the spacing material and replace it with the printing matter for the second color.
5. Remove, one at a time, all printing matter that was used for the first color and refill those areas with spaces and furniture.
6. Print the second color.

## PREPARING LINOLEUM BLOCKS FOR MULTICOLOR PRINTING

If you want to create your own design in two or more colors, linoleum cuts are the easiest to use. The following instructions will provide you with a set of cuts, one for each color.

1. Lock up the key block into the chase.
2. Make a lightly inked impression on the tympan.
3. Cut an .005″ sheet of clear acetate to the exact size of the printing paper.
4. Center the acetate over the tympan impression and position the paper margins. Attach gauge pins to the tympan to mark the position.
5. Make a fairly wet inked impression on the acetate.
6. Remove the key block from the chase and place an uncut linoleum block in its place. (I spray the linoleum with white paint for this purpose.)
7. With the acetate in position on the gauge pins, close the press. When you open it, you will have the required reverse imprint from which to cut the block for the next color.

Menu design for the Double Crown Club, 6″ x 3⅜″, by Gerard Meynell, London, 1924. An example of the elaborate use of border designs and ornaments with Italic type.

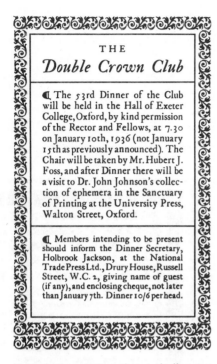

THE
*Double Crown Club*

❡ The 53rd Dinner of the Club will be held in the Hall of Exeter College, Oxford, by kind permission of the Rector and Fellows, at 7.30 on January 10th, 1936 (not January 15th as previously announced). The Chair will be taken by Mr. Hubert J. Foss, and after Dinner there will be a visit to Dr. John Johnson's collection of ephemera in the Sanctuary of Printing at the University Press, Walton Street, Oxford.

❡ Members intending to be present should inform the Dinner Secretary, Holbrook Jackson, at the National Trade Press Ltd., Drury House, Russell Street, W.C. 2, giving name of guest (if any), and enclosing cheque, not later than January 7th. Dinner 10/6 per head.

Two design choices for a similar purpose. The dinner announcement above uses a traditional border of fleurons. The one below is set in an off-center manner. Its three bold-face lines are in Condensed Grotesque type style.

# 62nd dinner

of the Double Crown Club will

be held 13 October 1937 at the

Cafe Royal at 7 for 7 15 pm

## Mr Christian Barman

will read a paper on

### Design in Timetables

Members intending to be present should

inform the Dinner Secretary, Holbrook Jackson

at the National Trade Press Ltd, Drury House

Russell Street WC2, giving name of guest

if any, and enclosing cheque (10s 6d per head)

not later than 11 October

8. For each additional color, an impression is transferred from the key block to an uncut lino block, repeating steps 2 to 7 each time.
9. When the impressions on the blocks have dried, indicate color areas on each block with Magic Markers. Areas without color (those which should not print) are then removed with linocut tools. An additional acetate impression of the key block should be made and set aside to be used in the actual printing. This impression should not be too heavily inked and should be as clean as possible.

## MULTICOLOR PRINTING FOR LINOCUTS

In color registration, it is necessary that all colors fall into their proper position on the printing paper and in relationship to one another.

Normally, in multicolor printing, the lightest color is printed first, and the key block, which has the darkest color, is printed last. However, should you want one color to dominate, or wish to overlap or overprint others, refer back to pages 34–35.

Proceed as follows:
1. Lock up the first linocut into the chase and put chase into the bed of the press.
2. Ink up in the color to be used and make a light impression on the tympan.
3. Take the sheet of acetate that was prepared and set aside (see 9, "Preparing Linoleum Blocks for Multicolor Printing") and position it over the color impression. This will show exactly how the key block will print over that color. Attach gauge pins to hold the acetate in that position.
4. Remove the acetate and insert the printing paper into the gauge pins. It should be in perfect alignment with the first impression. Print the entire run of that color and repeat all the steps for each additional color.

Before printing a new color, clean the ink disk and rollers of the previous ink.

## CLEAN-UP

Since ink rollers may be made of various materials, manufacturer's instructions should be followed in cleaning them. Usually, however, kerosene is recommended for gelatine rollers and Anchor Wash—R 228 for rubber rollers.

*(Facing page)* Two Christmas keepsakes designed by John Begg for Oxford University Press. *(Top)* Artist, Joseph Low; *(bottom)* artist, Emil Antonucci. Booklets such as these can be made on a platen press. The art can be printed from lino-, wood- or zinc cuts and hand-set type. Colored and textured papers for covers can be used to enhance the quality of these pieces.

## SAFETY

Ordinary caution should be used, as with any machinery. Make sure your hand is not in the press before pulling the lever down. Rubber gloves are recommended for all clean-up, since some people may be allergic to certain solvents.

## ADJUSTMENT TO PLATEN

The platen should always be perfectly parallel to the chase bed. In most cases this adjustment was made by the manufacturer, or, if the press was bought second-hand, by the previous owner. Should the platen, however, come loose or be out of alignment, the following procedure can be used to put it back into proper position.

Take four large pieces of type—capital M's are good for this—and secure them inside the four corners of the chase which is resting in the bed. They can be held in place by magnet locks which will eliminate having to fill the chase with furniture. Place a sheet of paper on the platen, close the press and take an impression. If none of the letters print add more sheets under the tympan and take another impression. By the M's that now do not print, you will know exactly which side of the platen is out of parallel alignment. Correction is made by gradually tightening the corresponding bolt behind the platen. This will involve a readjustment of the other bolts also, but all must be done slowly and gradually.

Printed pages of booklet ready for assembling and stapling. One staple in the center of the fold is sufficient. Two staples attach the pages to the cover along the upper and lower parts of the fold.

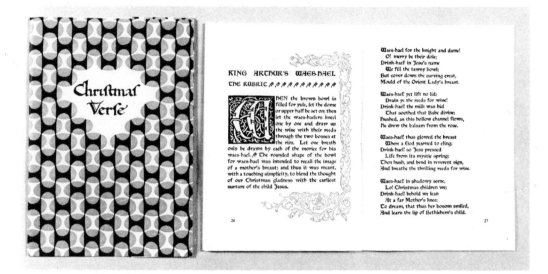

Christmas keepsake designed by John Begg for Oxford University Press. Page was set with William Morris type, initial, and decoration. Printed in two colors, blue and black.

# To Make a Booklet

An eight-page booklet can be made on the platen press by using just one sheet of paper. Four pages are printed at the same time on one side of the paper. When that side is dry, it is turned over and the other four pages are printed. The sheet is then folded and trimmed.

For the type to be in correct position on the pages, an imposition is followed. To see how this imposition works, fold a sheet of paper in half, then in half again. With the folded sides at left and top, number the side of each fold from 1 to 8. Unfold the paper and check it against the diagram **A**—it should read exactly the same. Before unfolding the paper, if you had cut the fold-over at the top, you would have had eight pages marked in the correct order. When preparing the lock-up, follow the form layout as shown in the diagram **B.** This layout is mirror-image and will print out to the correct imposition. By checking the proof, you will be able to correct any type that may have been put in wrong side up or down. The finished printed pages can be inserted into a cover of heavier stock and all held together with staples. Additional eight-page sections can of course be used to enlarge the booklet.

By printing on only one side of the sheet, using two or more of the four pages, and then folding the sheet in the same manner as above, a "French fold" is obtained which enhances the finished print. This is ideal for printing greeting cards and announcements.

Imposition for an 8-page booklet. One sheet of paper is printed on both sides. Arrows indicate tops of pages.

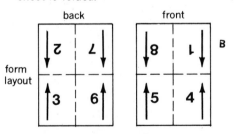

In diagram **A,** the numbers indicate the imposition of the pages so that they will run consecutively when the sheet is folded.

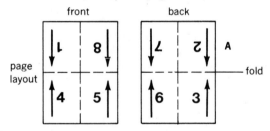

Diagram **B** shows the form in the chase set up mirror-image so that the pages will print according to the imposition in diagram **A.**

# *Glossary*

**Baren**—An instrument for hand-rubbing prints.

**Bench Hook**—A device used to hold a wood or linoleum block while cutting.

**Brayer**—A soft rubber roller mounted on a handle and used to roll out ink and to transfer it to the printing surface.

**Character**—A single piece of type, such as a letter, figure, punctuation mark, etc.

**Chase**—A cast-iron frame which holds a form for printing on the platen press.

**End-grain**—The surface of a block of wood that is exposed when the wood is cut directly across the grain.

**Engraving**—Cutting a design into wood with sharp tools, usually gravers and scorpers.

**Form**—Type and cuts, locked up for printing.

**Furniture**—Metal or wood spacing material used to fill in open spaces around type and/or cuts.

**Galley**—A rectangular metal tray in which type can be set.

**Gripper Bar**—A means of holding the paper in position for printing on the proof press.

**Imposing Stone**—Any smooth or level surface on which type and/or cuts are assembled.

**Impression**—A print made from an inked block by pressure.

**Impression Roller**—On the proof press, the cylinder that presses the paper against the inked printing surface.

**India Ink**—A black ink used for drawing and painting.

**Ink Slab**—A large piece of glass upon which ink may be rolled out.

**Key Block**—The block used as a guide for positioning other blocks in color registration. Usually it prints in the darkest color.

**Linocut**—A linoleum block from which a design has been carved in relief for printing. Also a print taken from such a block.

**Linoleum Block**—A piece of Battleship linoleum mounted usually on plywood.

**Lock-up**—The fastening of material to be printed within a chase on the platen press, or securing it in a fixed position on the proof press.

**Magnet Locks**—Locks used to hold type in place on the proof press.

**Pica**—Unit of measurement used in measuring type areas. One pica equals 1/6 of an inch.

**Plate**—A block, cut, or other material upon which an image has been carved for the purpose of printing.

**Platen**—The flat metal surface on which paper is placed for printing in a platen press.

**Point**—Unit of measurement designating type size. One point equals 1/72 of an inch.

**Posterboard**—Cardboard about ⅛″ thick.

**Proof**—A trial print made for the purpose of being studied and corrected.

**Quoins**—Metal wedges or rectangular shapes. They take up any slack left by spacing material and apply pressure.

**Register**—To print an impression so that each color falls exactly in the correct position in relation to other colors on the printing sheet.

**Relief Printing**—A method of printing in which the surface to be printed is raised, thus being higher than the surrounding non-printing areas. Also called "letterpress."

**Solvent**—A solution used for cleaning brayers and rollers, type and cuts.

**Type**—A single cast metal body with a letter, number, punctuation mark, or other character in relief.

**Type Cabinet**—A piece of furniture for storing cases of hand type.

**Type High**—The height of type, .918″.

**Woodcut**—A flat plank or block of wood on which an image has been carved in relief for printing; also a print taken from such a block.

**Wood Engraving**—A process of engraving a design on a polished block of end-grain wood; the strength of the surface permits the cutting of delicate lines in any direction. Also a print obtained from such a process.

**Zinc Cut**—A printing plate onto which a black and white line print, drawing, or type has been photographically transferred. The areas not to print are etched away, leaving a raised surface for inking.

# Bibliography

Cleeton, Glen U., and Pitkin, Charles W., *GENERAL PRINTING,* McKnight & McKnight Publishing Co., Bloomington, Ill., 1953

Green, Peter, *INTRODUCING SURFACE PRINTING,* Watson-Guptill Publications, Inc., New York, N.Y., 1968

Karshan, Donald H., *PICASSO LINOCUTS 1958–1963,* Tudor Publishing Co., New York, N.Y., 1968 (The Computer Applications Inc. Collection)

Lee, Marshall, *BOOKMAKING: The Illustrated Guide to Design and Production,* R. R. Bowker Co., New York, N.Y., 1965

Rothenstein, Michael, *LINOCUTS AND WOODCUTS: A Complete Block Printing Handbook,* Watson-Guptill Publications, Inc., New York, N.Y., 1963

Sternberg, Harry, *WOODCUT,* Pitman Publishing Corp., New York, N.Y., 1962

*ARTIST'S PROOF, The Annual of Prints and Printmaking.* Published by the Pratt Graphic Center, an extension of Pratt Institute, Brooklyn, N.Y., and by Barre Publishers, Barre, Mass.

Linocut by Martin Silverman

# Suppliers

**General:**

The Craftool Co.
1421 W. 240th St.
Harbor City, Calif. 90710

Graphic Chemical & Ink Co.
728 North Yale Ave.
Villa Park, Ill. 60181

M. Grumbacher Inc.
460 West 34th St.
New York, N.Y. 10001

Rembrandt Graphic Arts Co., Inc.
Stockton, N.J. 08559

Yasutomo & Co.
24 California St.
San Francisco, Calif. 94111

Sam Flax Company
25 East 28th St.
New York, N.Y. 10016

**Papers:**

Aiko's Art Materials Import
714 Wabash Ave.
Chicago, Ill. 60611

Andrews-Nelson-Whitehead
7 Laight St.
New York, N.Y. 10013

Crown Zellerbach Corp.
1 Bush St.
San Francisco, Calif. 94119

Strathmore Paper Co.
West Springfield, Mass. 01089

Technical Papers Corp.
729 Boylston St.
Boston, Mass. 02116

**Presses:**

Nolan-Jampol, Inc.
Rome, N.Y. 13440
(Proof Press)

United States Forge & Foundry Co.
Machinery Division
Pulaski, N.Y. 13142

**Cutting & Engraving Tools:**

J. Johnson & Co.
33 Matinecock Ave.
Port Washington, N.Y. 11050
(Type high wood blocks)

Frank Mittermier Inc.
2577 East Tremont Ave.
Bronx, N.Y. 10465

**Type:**

American Wood Type Mfg. Co.
42–25 Ninth St.
Long Island City, N.Y. 11101

Judson Graphics, Inc.
150 Varick St.
New York, N.Y. 10013
(This firm sells type by the line.)

# School Directory

The following schools offer courses in printmaking. All schools operate year-round except those marked with an asterisk, which are summer workshops only. Since printmaking is so popular and widely taught, no attempt was made to include universities and colleges. For further information, write to the school direct.

Brooks Institute
School of Fine Art
2020 Alameda Padre Serra
Santa Barbara, California 93103

San Francisco Art Institute
800 Chestnut St.
San Francisco, California 94133

Laguna Beach School of Art & Design
630 Laguna Canyon Rd.
Laguna Beach, California 92651

*Black Hawk School of Art
Black Hawk, Colorado 80427

Hartford Art School
University of Hartford
Bloomfield Ave.
West Hartford, Connecticut 06117

Paier School of Art
6 Prospect Court
Hamden, Connecticut 06511

Silvermine College of Art
Silvermine, Connecticut Rd.
New Canaan, Connecticut 06840

Rehoboth Art League
Henlopen Acres
Rehoboth Beach, Delaware 19971

Corcoran School of Art
17th & New York Ave. N.W.,
Washington, D.C. 20016

Chase School of Art
1310 Bay Rd.
Sarasota, Florida 33579

Chicago Academy of Fine Art
84–86 East Randolph St.
Chicago, Illinois 60601

The School of Art
Institute of Chicago
Michigan Ave. & Adams St.
Chicago, Illinois 60603

Fort Wayne Art Institute, Inc.
1026 West Berry St.
Fort Wayne, Indiana 46804

Herron School of Art
Indiana University
1701 North Pennsylvania
Indianapolis, Indiana 46202

Art Center Assoc.
Louisvile School of Art
2111 South First St.
Louisville, Kentucky 40208

Louisiana Polytechnic Institute
Dept. of Art & Architecture
Tech. Station
Ruston, Louisiana 71360

*Haystack Mountain School of Crafts
Deer Isle, Maine 04627

School of Fine & Applied Arts
93 High & 97 Spring Sts.
Portland, Maine 04101

Maryland Institute
College of Art
1300 Mount Royal Ave.
Baltimore, Maryland 21217

The Maryland School
of Art & Design
932 Philadelphia Ave.
Silver Springs, Maryland 20901

The Art Institute of Boston
718 Beacon St.
Boston, Massachusetts 02215

Boston Center for Adult Education
5 Commonwealth Ave.
Boston, Massachusetts 02116

Cambridge Center for Adult Education
42 Brattle St.
Cambridge, Massachusetts 02138

New England School of Art
285 Huntington Ave.
Boston, Massachusetts 02115

*Provincetown Workshop
492 Commercial St.
Provincetown, Massachusetts 02657

School of the Museum of Fine Arts
230 Fenway
Boston, Massachusetts 02115

School of the Worcester Art Museum
55 Salisbury St.
Worcester, Massachusetts 01608

The Art School of the Society
of Arts & Crafts
245 East Kirby
Detroit, Michigan 48202

Kendall School of Design
1110 College N.E.,
Grand Rapids, Michigan 49503

The Minneapolis School of Art
200 East 25 St.
Minneapolis, Minnesota 55404

St. Paul Art Center School
30 East 10 St.
St. Paul, Minnesota 55101

School of the Associated Arts
344 Summit Ave.
St. Paul, Minnesota 55101

Kansas City Art Institute
4415 Warwick Blvd.
Kansas City, Missouri 64111

Newark School of Fine
& Industrial Arts
550 High St.
Newark, New Jersey 07102

Ridgewood School of Art
83 Chestnut St.
Ridgewood, New Jersey 07450

El Portal Institute for Fine Arts
745 North Alameda Ave.
Las Cruces, New Mexico 87701

Art Students League of N.Y.
215 West 57 St.
New York, New York 10019

The Cooper Union School
of Art & Architecture
Cooper Sq.
New York, New York 10003

Educational Alliance Art School
197 East Broadway
New York, New York 10002

Henry St. Settlement
School of Art & Pottery
265 Henry St.
New York, New York 10002

New York-Phoenix School of Design
160 Lexington Ave.
New York, New York 10016

Pratt Graphics Center
831 Broadway
New York, New York 10003

Pratt Institute
The Art School
200 Grand Ave.
Brooklyn, New York 11205

Rochester Institute of Technology,
College of Fine & Applied Arts,
School of Art & Design,
School for American Craftsmen,
Lomb Memorial Dr.
Rochester, New York 14623

School of Visual Arts
209–213 East 23 St.
New York, New York 10010

Syracuse University
School of Art
309 University Pl.
Syracuse, New York 13210

Westchester Art Workshop
County Center
White Plains, New York 10606

The Art Academy of Cincinnati
Eden Park
Cincinnati, Ohio 45202

The Cleveland Institute of Art
11141 East Blvd.
Cleveland, Ohio 44106

Cooper School of Art
2112 Euclid Ave.
Cleveland, Ohio 44115

School of the Dayton Art Institute
Forest & Riverview Aves.
Dayton, Ohio 45405

Museum Art School
651 Northwest Culpepper Terr.
Portland, Oregon 97210

The Academy of the Arts
107 Sixth St.
Pittsburgh, Pennsylvania 15222

Moore College of Art
20 & Race Sts.
Philadelphia, Pennsylvania 19103

The Pennsylvania Academy of the Fine Art
Broad & Cherry Sts.
Philadelphia, Pennsylvania 19002

Philadelphia College of Art
Broad & Pine Sts.
Philadelphia, Pennsylvania 19101

Tyler School of Art
Temple University
Beech & Penrose Aves.
Philadelphia, Pennsylvania 19126

Rhode Island School of Design
2 College St.
Providence, Rhode Island 02903

Richland Art School
Columbia Museum of Art
1112 Bull St.
Columbia, South Carolina 29201

Memphis Academy of Art
Overton Park
Memphis, Tennessee 38112

Dallas Art Institute
2523 McKinney Ave.
Dallas, Texas 75201

Museum School of Art
Houston Museum of Fine Arts
1001 Bisonnet
Houston, Texas 77005

*Southern Vermont Art Center
Manchester, Vermont 05255

Hampton Institute
Hampton, Virginia 23364

Holden School of Fine & Applied Arts
215 East High St.
Charlottesville, Virginia 22902

Cornish School of Art
710 East Roy St.
Seattle, Washington 98102

Art Originals Gallery & School
237 East Ryan Rd.
Oak Creek, Wisconsin 53154

Layton School of Art
1362 North Prospect Ave.
Milwaukee, Wisconsin 53202